EFFECTIVE
TAEKWON-DO
SPARRING

EFFECTIVE TAEKWON-DO SPARRING

Master Jim Hogan and James Home

THE CROWOOD PRESS

First published in 2009 by
The Crowood Press Ltd
Ramsbury, Marlborough
Wiltshire SN8 2HR

www.crowood.com

British Library Cataloguing-in-Publication Data
A catalogue record for this book is available from the British Library.

ISBN 978 1 84797 134 0

Disclaimer
Please note that the authors and the publisher of this book are not responsible in any manner whatsoever for any damage or injury of any kind that may result from practising, or applying, the principles, ideas, techniques and/or following the instructions/information described in this publication. Since the physical activities described in this book may be too strenuous in nature for some readers to engage in safely, it is essential that a doctor be consulted before undertaking any training or sparring.

All the photographs in this book were taken by Tim J. Rumble of Britannia Photographic Ltd.

Typeset in Plantin by Bookcraft, Stroud, Gloucestershire

Printed and bound in Malaysia by Times Offset (M) Sdn Bhd

Contents

Preface

Some people love to fight – they revel in the excitement of meeting new opponents, testing themselves against more skilled fighters, taking risks to score with a winning technique ... and some people don't. For some, free sparring is an anxious experience, perhaps they just aren't that competitive or perhaps they fear injury, but whatever the reason, they are uncomfortable in a sparring situation and their anxiety constrains their performance. This book addresses both groups. If you are an enthusiastic fighter but perhaps aren't winning as often or as well as you would like, then maybe you need to fight smarter. If you lack confidence and find yourself 'freezing' then you probably need to be more in control of yourself and your opponent.

The starting point for this book is the recognition that sparring is not merely an extension of what you learn standing in line in class at your martial arts club. Yes, it is built on the blocking, punching and kicking techniques in the formal syllabus but these fundamentals need to be adapted for the sparring arena. This book seeks to help club-level fighters in Taekwon-Do and other similar martial arts to think about their sparring in more detail, to make those adaptations and thereby make their sparring more effective.

Master Jim Hogan, VII Degree
James Home, IV Degree

1 Introduction

The Need for this Book

Taekwon-Do, like most Asian martial arts, has many aspects that attract students for many different reasons. Some are drawn to the physical training, some to the perfection of martial techniques, some to the wider moral and ethical principles of self-discipline, self-improvement and mutual respect … and some to fighting. But for whatever reasons people come to it, Taekwon-Do exists and prospers as a self-defence art and every aspect of Taekwon-Do training relates back to this core purpose: effective self-defence. The role of sparring in pursuit of this goal is therefore crucial since it provides the best test of how effective techniques are for individual students in realistic (yet controlled) combat. Or at least that is what it should be – in practice, sparring often falls far short of this goal because many people find it difficult to transfer the techniques that they have learnt 'formally' in class into the sparring arena.

Why should this be? Two reasons: first, there is a difference between how to perform, for example, a powerful side kick that can break through boards of wood as part of a grade promotion test and how to deliver a fast, deceptive side kick that can sneak in under an opponent's guard. The former requires an understanding of how to generate maximum penetrative power against a static target, while the latter is more concerned with how to seize a fleeting opportunity against a moving target. Both are valid and, indeed, the 'formal' understanding is a prerequisite for the practical application, but they are nonetheless different and require different approaches in their teaching. While there is an 'ideal', technical side

kick that everyone can aspire to when performing the technique in isolation, multiple variables come into play when sparring – each individual needs both to develop a personal style that best suits him and then to adapt that to rapidly changing circumstances. This is not something that an instructor can teach a class of students all at the same time; he can show examples, for instance, of sparring combinations and criticize students' sparring performances, but, ultimately, individuals must take responsibility for applying what they learn in their sparring. And that is one of the goals of the book: to get you, the reader, thinking about how you fight more deeply than you may have done in the past and to use this analysis to constantly refine and improve your sparring.

Secondly, while the above describes a need for a process there is also a need for content. The fundamentals on which effective sparring is based differ significantly from the formal syllabus of Taekwon-Do and other similar martial arts. Basics such as stance, guard and movement need to be revisited and adapted; this book tries to set down in some detail what fundamentals you need to change and why.

In addressing these two needs the book does not seek to provide a comprehensive manual on the myriad aspects of sparring, rather it seeks to offer a framework that you can use to improve your sparring by making it more effective.

Who Should Read It?

The book is aimed squarely at the beginner to intermediate-level martial artist who trains at his local club and possibly enters local and national competitions. While it may be of value to more experienced fighters, with its strong emphasis on fundamentals the book's primary focus is on the club-level martial artist who is conscious of that gap between his performance in class and when he is sparring.

It is written from the perspective of Taekwon-Do as taught by the ITF (International Tae-kwon-Do Federation). Taekwon-Do is a Korean self-defence art created some fifty years ago and is now one of the world's most popular martial arts, that practises continuous, semi-free sparring where both hand and foot techniques can be applied to legitimate targets 'above the belt'. Under this regime, fighters are free to kick and punch (with a degree of control and while wearing protective gloves and footwear) to the head and the body until they are stopped by the referee due to some infringement of the rules or the end of a round. Since this format, with slight variations, is shared by other martial arts, this book is therefore equally applicable to students of, for instance, karate, kung fu and kickboxing, as it is to those of ITF Taekwon-Do.

The Structure of the Book

The book is divided into three sections that reflect the authors' view of the progressive nature of the teaching of sparring.

Part I   Fundamentals

The bedrock of effective sparring is correct body positioning and footwork, and these are broken down into the core components of stance, guard and movement. The importance of these elements cannot be emphasized enough and they are covered in considerable detail before they are brought together in one of the most neglected aspects of sparring: defence. Again, defence is covered in some detail to reinforce its importance and to try to get you to put it at the heart of your sparring.

Part II   Core Techniques

What makes a particular technique effective in sparring? How is it best adapted from the class to the ring? How can you train to improve your technique? This section answers these and related questions by examining some core techniques in all of the major categories (that is, hand techniques, lead-leg kicks, rear-leg kicks and jumping kicks) and providing training drills to help you to develop them. The use of sparring drills is key to your future progress because it is the most effective way to refine sparring techniques: by using those provided as a template you can go on to develop your own drills for your specific needs.

Part III   Strategy

This final section looks at some of the more strategic aspects of sparring, such as how to assess your opponent, how to create openings, effective attacking combinations and counter-attacks.

Each section is divided into chapters that each cover a single topic, such as stance, jumping kicks and creating openings, and, within each chapter, photographs of the authors are used extensively to illustrate techniques in some detail. These photographs are your principal study aid because they (generally) show the performance of a technique from start to finish, allowing you to study the body position and footwork leading up to the technique. This is of particular importance given the strong emphasis placed on these fundamentals throughout and, where necessary, a red marker has been used as a fixed point in a series of photographs the better to illustrate the distance travelled and the direction being followed.

How to Use this Book

Each section is dependent on a good understanding of its predecessor (and, in the case of the first section, of each chapter) and you will therefore get the most out of it by tackling it strictly in the order in which it is presented.

As you approach each new topic, try not to be in too much of a hurry and try to 'realize' the points made rather than just to read them. This 'realization' is necessary because, from your current standpoint, you may not agree with many of the arguments made, for example, in the case of stance. If you have been training and sparring for a couple of years you will be used to working off your own stance and may not initially see that there is any need to change it. But we hope that you will find the arguments for a change of stance persuasive after you have considered them, but even this is not enough. If you are going to make

fundamental changes to your sparring style then you need truly to believe the reasons behind them and you must therefore experience some actual improvement by changing your stance. The effort of reading is only the start – you must not only practise the technique until you can perform it adequately, but you must also use it in your sparring sufficiently to be able to recognize it as an improvement or otherwise.

Ultimately, sparring style is personal and you should use the book to make your own style more effective by a process of development rather than revolution. Take your time with the book, think about the points it makes, try them out, play around with them and then incorporate what works for you.

Part I
Fundamentals

The foundation of effective Taekwon-Do sparring is the same as that of the martial art of which it is a part – strong basics – and there are two core elements upon which everything else rests: a good defence and correct movement. We cannot emphasize the importance of these fundamentals strongly enough, and we have presented them here in particular detail, not merely to help you to learn about stance, guard, movement and defence but so that you may properly grasp their importance and put them at the heart of your sparring.

2 Sparring Basics

Before you even consider 'how' to spar more effectively it is essential that you have a clear view of what you are trying to achieve. Why? Because many students set themselves unrealistic goals; it is not about turning yourself into a martial arts superhero but making the best use of your abilities in a clearly defined and controlled set of circumstances. Your starting point must therefore be the rules and boundaries of free sparring that dictate your core objectives and the strategies that you must adopt to achieve them.

Style

Taekwon-Do, like an increasing number of more 'traditional' martial arts, practises semi-contact, continuous, free sparring. *Semi-contact* is a term used essentially to distinguish normal club and competition sparring from 'full-contact' sparring where techniques are executed at full power with the ultimate goal of incapacitating your opponent. While there is much to be said for the full-contact regime as a sterner and perhaps more realistic test of martial arts skills, with its intense physical demands and increased risk of injury, it is not appropriate for the majority of martial artists. Equally, while 'no-contact' or 'touch' sparring, where techniques stop just short of the target making no or only very light contact, can be very skilful and dynamic when performed at a high level, for most martial artists it lacks realism. Semi-contact is therefore a compromise between these two extremes, where the maximum amount of realism is achieved with the minimum risk of injury, and in Taekwon-Do sparring an effective

technique (and one that will 'score') is therefore defined as one that is:

- executed correctly at the appropriate distance
- dynamic with speed, power and accuracy
- controlled and executed at a valid target

These definitions are, of course, open to some interpretation. Yet they are worth thinking over so that they become your goal and so that you try to deliver proper Taekwon-Do techniques with as much speed and power as you can while still being able to control their final impact and avoid injuring your opponent. In practice, it is difficult to get those 'clean shots', but this should be your aim since these would be the most effective techniques were they delivered at full power in a real self-defence situation and, in any case, competition judges will score them much more readily than flurries of unfocused kicks and punches.

Continuous sparring means that the fight continues without interruption unless the referee intervenes because of some infraction of the rules or it is the end of the round. This differs significantly from the 'single-point' sparring practised by some martial arts, such as more traditional styles of Karate where the fight is stopped if a point is scored. Again, much can be said for single-point sparring and, in particular, the way that it encourages great accuracy and fast counter-attacking skills – both aspects that can usefully be incorporated into Taekwon-Do sparring. However, a 'sudden-death' regime requires a very different approach from continuous sparring where your strategy needs to encompass the full duration of each round (usually one or two 2min rounds in Taekwon-Do), and where pace and defence become important considerations.

Finally, *free* sparring is a relative term in that, although there are rules regarding, for instance, the levels of contact and allowable target areas (*see* below), fighters should be able to draw upon the full range of techniques in their armoury. This is particularly the case in Taekwon-Do with its strong emphasis on aerial techniques that can be challenging enough to execute correctly in class, let alone when sparring. So in order to encourage fighters to demonstrate their proficiency in Taekwon-Do and not just rely on 'basic' scoring techniques, more points are awarded for jumping attacks resulting in fighters using a wider range of techniques, which, in turn, makes Taekwon-Do sparring so exciting to participate in and to watch.

Rules

Within this semi-contact, continuous, free-sparring style there are relatively few rules that the competitor must follow.

Clothing and Equipment

Clothing will be as dictated by your association – in ITF Taekwon-Do it is always the regulation white training uniform (*dobok*) and belt, signifying your grade, whether training at a club or entering a competition. Minimum safety equipment regulations will also vary but, at club level, students must always wear padded hand and foot protectors that are substantial enough to offer significant protection to your opponent, but not so much so that they greatly increase the size of your attacking tool as with 'heavy' boxing gloves. There are many good makes of martial arts sparring equipment – Hyashi Top Ten and Macho are two of the most popular in Taekwon-Do. These basic components can be supplemented by a range of optional equipment, some of which will be compulsory in competitions, including:

- groin guard (males)
- breast protector (females)
- mouth guard
- head guard (recommended at all times for juniors when sparring)
- shin protectors
- forearm protectors

Target Area

See opposite.

Faults

The referee will pause the fight and deduct a point from a competitor for:

- loss of temper
- misconduct from a competitor towards an opponent
- biting or scratching
- knee, elbow or head attacks
- attacks to a fallen opponent
- excessive contact

Warnings

The referee will pause the fight and issue a warning to a competitor for:

- attack to an illegal target
- stepping out of the ring area with both feet
- falling (touching the ground with any part of the body other than the feet)
- holding, grabbing or pushing
- sweeping an opponent's feet
- intentionally avoiding sparring
- celebrating a technique
- feigning injury after receiving an attack

At the end of the fight a point is deducted for each complete set of three warnings issued to a competitor.

Disqualification

The referee will immediately stop the fight and disqualify a competitor for:

Target Areas

For safety reasons, the target area is restricted to the head, neck and trunk above the navel at the front and the sides of the head and body – striking to the back of the body, head or neck or at any point below the navel is not allowed. This target area is divided into two sections:

High section comprising targets above the shoulder line and in front of a line drawn vertically behind the ear.

Middle section comprising the body below the shoulder line, above the navel and in front of a vertical line drawn from the armpit to the waist.

- misconduct towards the referee and/or ignoring his instructions
- full-contact attack
- accumulating three minus points directly during the fight
- being under the influence of drink or drugs

Scoring

Points are awarded for valid attack techniques to the target area as follows:
- one point for:
  — hand attack to mid or high section
  — foot attack to mid section
- two points for:
  — foot attack to high section
  — jumping or flying foot attack to mid section
  — jumping or flying hand attack to high section
- three points for:
  — jumping or flying foot attack to high section.

(A 'jumping or flying' attack is deemed successful when both of the attacker's feet are still off the ground at the moment of impact.)

Objectives

Your objective in free sparring is to win by scoring more points than your opponent. Simple! But the rules and the scoring system play a large part in determining how best to achieve that objective in the most efficient and therefore the most effective manner.

Clearly all fights are different in that you have to react to an unpredictable opponent (although recognizing predictable actions and 'training' your opponent to behave in a predictable way are key weapons in your armoury that are covered in later chapters), but the sparring format gives rise to three fundamental principles that form the basis of effective sparring.

Fight within the Rules

It really serves no purpose for you to deliberately break any of the rules and receive any unnecessary warnings or faults, not only would you be working against yourself by incurring minus penalty points, but, more importantly, you would not be fully in control. Consider this scenario: you are on the receiving end of a strong punch and you feel that your opponent was using excessive contact but the referee has not intervened, so in your anger you determine to get even and deliberately punch your opponent with full force. Even if the referee does not see the technique properly and does not therefore give a warning, while you may hope that your opponent will now think twice about using excessive contact again, he may well be thinking that he has the advantage since he has clearly made you react. He could be thinking that you are to be treated with respect, but he could also be thinking that you are easy to rile, to make lose control and therefore make mistakes. However, if your response is to tighten up your defence, show that you are not intimidated by standing your ground and reply with some good, clean scoring shots (and, yes, perhaps use a little more contact than you might ordinarily), then, whatever else your opponent may be thinking, it will not be that he has gained the advantage. You must have self-control to spar well, and fighting within the rules shows your opponent that you have it.

Aim to Score Points

A statement of the obvious? Not if you have any experience in judging sparring competitions where you will frequently see a great deal of activity from fighters resulting in relatively few points. Of course, you cannot attack effectively all the time – you need to react to your opponent, you need to feint, you need to defend – but try not to waste effort in attacks that are never going to succeed. You must score points to win, and attacks that have no chance of success – because they are

well out of range, not on target or are not being used to set up a more effective attack – are wasted effort. Try to focus on delivering scoring techniques rather than just being 'busy'. Equally, it is not enough to rely on counter-attacking (which can be an effective strategy in 'single-point' sparring): you are unlikely to score more points than your opponent by merely answering his attacks – you must put your opponent under pressure by going forward.

Avoid Getting Hit

An even more obvious point? Maybe, but if this book has a single, overriding message then it is this: *a good defence is essential for effective sparring.*

Again, if you have watched or judged sparring competitions you will have noticed that (particularly among less experienced fighters) a poor defence is more often the reason for a scoring attack than the quality of the technique. No matter how fast, strong and varied your attacking skills may be, a good defence gives you three key advantages before you even score a point:

- *Winning is easier* – regardless of how good your opponent may be, the fewer scoring techniques he can land on you, the fewer you have to land on him to win.
- *Your opponent must work harder* – if your defence is the stronger then your opponent must work harder and perhaps try things outside his comfort zone to prevail; this creates more openings for you.
- *Your confidence increases* – once you begin to develop a good defence you will feel under less pressure and more able to think strategically, and that will, in turn, increase your confidence and your effectiveness.

In summary, effective Taekwon-Do sparring proceeds from a good defence that allows you to pursue an attacking strategy with the least risk to yourself, and this is what this book offers.

3 Stance

The absolute bedrock of effective sparring is a good stance. Everything else – how you move, how you attack and defend, your attitude and your self-confidence – is underpinned by your stance: your foot position, your weight distribution and your orientation.

Perhaps you are thinking that this is a statement of the obvious, that your stance suits you well enough and that what you need to learn are better techniques and strategy. Perhaps you are also somewhat irritated to hear such emphasis placed on stance when it is something that is stressed so much in Taekwon-Do and other martial arts with their wide variety of stances – what more is there to learn about stances? However, we regard a good sparring stance as fundamental to effective sparring and therefore to the rest of this book and we encourage you to study this chapter carefully and try to relate its messages to any shortcomings or areas for improvement in your current sparring. Do you have difficulty moving out of the way of attack? Do you get hit frequently? Are you too susceptible to counter-attacks? Are your attacks often out of range? Do your opponents seem to see you coming? Are you too tense? All of these and other issues are addressed at their core by stance, and free sparring requires a different approach to stance than that used in the formal stances you have been taught.

Why Change?

When you learn formal stances in Taekwon-Do or other martial arts emphasizing the correct execution of techniques and pre-arranged patterns (such as *tul* in Taekwon-Do or *kata* in Karate), the stances that you learn are introduced to cover the full ranges of weight distribution and body position. Each stance serves specific purposes, thus l-stance is a good defensive stance but it can limit your options for attack (*see* first sequence on page 16).

Similarly, a strong walking stance is an excellent position through which to maximize the power of a punch, but not the best from which to move away quickly (*see* second sequence on page 16).

Clearly different stances will be appropriate in different situations, not only in your structured classes but also in your sparring – there is no one 'correct' stance, each has its advantages and disadvantages. The 'good' sparring stance is not a 'better' stance than the l-stance or walking stance, rather it draws on the body of knowledge about stances and footwork to provide a 'compromise' stance that becomes your 'default' from which you can defend and attack and, if necessary, move into and out of other stances. What is the most effective compromise for effective Taekwon-Do sparring? There are two principal requirements.

Defence

As discussed previously, a good defence is essential for effective sparring, so the sparring stance must offer protection of the key target areas, allowing you to stand your ground behind your defence or back off, as the situation demands.

Mobility

Equally importantly, you need to be dynamic in your stance (that is, able to make small rapid movements to avoid presenting a static target) as well as able to move easily in any direction to defend, to counter-attack or to launch an attack.

Limitations of L-Stance

The classic, side-facing l-stance offers good protection for the body and with most of the weight on the rear leg …

… it is easy to launch front-leg kicks such as the front-snap kick but …

… a rear-leg kick, such as a turning kick, requires all the weight to be shifted on to the front leg.

Limitations of Walking Stance

A deep walking stance can generate power in a stepping punch, but …

… to move away from a counter-attack the whole body must be raised before you can step away …

… creating a delay that your opponent can exploit.

Basic Sparring Stance

The basic sparring stance shown here meets all of these requirements and has been developed from three principal sources:

- Master Hogan's early experience in boxing
- Master Hogan's extensive experience of Taekwon-Do sparring and coaching at international level
- current trends in Taekwon-Do and other styles of continuous, semi-contact, free sparring

How to Form the Basic Sparring Stance

This stance (*see* sequence on page 18) needs to become second nature to you – your default position when sparring – and you need to be able to form it instantly when under pressure. However, at the outset, this stance is far from natural for most people and it will require a lot of practice and awareness of the 'bad' habits that are so easy to revert to. It is therefore most important that you fully understand the advantages of the stance so that your self-correction (and there will be lots of it) has an argument behind it that you believe in. The principal components of the stance are examined in detail.

Foot Position

The position of the feet is of paramount importance and is, in fact, a slight modification of the classic boxing stance. As with boxers, the starting point is to keep the feet at least shoulder-width apart to provide the optimum combination of balance and mobility. Similarly, one foot is placed forward of the other (typically the left if you are right-handed and vice versa) to give greater all-round stability. Where Taekwon-Do sparring differs from boxing is, of course, in the use of kicks that require fighters to attack from a greater range and to use longer strides in their footwork to avoid the longer-range techniques.

This difference is highlighted when we look at WTF (World Taekwon-Do Federation, an alternative Taekwon-Do organization) sparring. WTF practise a different style of sparring from the ITF, where high-section punches are not allowed and there is consequently a much greater (scoring) emphasis on kicking that in turn has resulted in a particularly long stance. ITF Taekwon-Do and other sparring styles which allow both punching and kicking to all target areas need to occupy the middle ground the better to cope with both short- and long-range fighting with a slightly longer and wider stance than the standard boxing stance (*see* first sequence on page 19).

Of equal importance to the length and width of the stance are the actual positions of the feet which *must* be facing forward and turned slightly inward to allow a more natural body orientation (*see* the section on body orientation below). This positioning is absolutely critical to the success of the stance, since it not only provides the optimum starting position from which to launch forward rapidly like a sprinter from the blocks, but it also allows you to move in any direction while maintaining your balance (*see* Chapter 5). However, of all of the aspects of the sparring stance this is the hardest to master since there is a common tendency for the rear foot to turn out when the feet are in this position and this is exacerbated when in a sparring situation, where your natural instincts are to lean back away from the source of potential danger and find yourself in more of an l-stance (*see* second sequence on page 19).

While it certainly is not the case that you should never be in the l-stance when sparring, the difficulty is in forcing yourself to return to your sparring stance from what you instinctively feel to be your 'natural' defensive position when you are under pressure. This is an extremely common problem and you must try to be aware of its happening and make a conscious effort to correct yourself at all times – constant practice and correction are needed to create a new 'natural' stance.

How to Form the Basic Sparring Stance

Start by standing in a normal parallel stance with the feet shoulder-width apart and facing forward.

Take one natural step forward with your lead leg …

… then turn both your feet slightly (10 or 15 degrees at most) towards your rear-leg side.

Turn your upper body so that it is at the same angle as your feet …

… and bend both knees, dropping your body straight down until your rear heel lifts slightly off the ground and you can feel your weight predominantly on the balls of your feet.

You have now formed the basic sparring stance.

Sparring Stance Length Comparison

The WTF sparring stance is slightly deeper than the …

… ITF sparring stance, which sits between it and …

… the standard Western boxing stance.

The Common Tendency to Revert to L-Stance

It is common to start out in a good sparring stance …

… but when under pressure from your opponent (particularly when retreating) …

19

… you can find yourself reverting to an l-stance.

Weight Distribution

To continue the comparison with the sprinter in the blocks, in order for you to launch yourself forward (and, indeed, to move in any other direction) you need to avoid being flat-footed and have most of your weight on the balls of your feet, which means that your weight must be distributed slightly more towards the front foot, which, in turn, will make the heel of the back foot rise slightly off the ground. Rather than express this in terms of the percentages of your weight on the front and on the back foot, it is easier just to feel when it is right for you.

As with the foot position, you need to be constantly on your guard to recognize and correct the 'natural' tendency to shift your weight more towards your back foot, particularly when you are under pressure from your opponent (*see* sequence below).

Knee Flexion

With the feet in the right position and your body weight slightly forward, the comparison with the sprinter yields one final component to your sparring stance – that there is a slight flexion or bend of the knees. Not only does this ensure that you will be able to move your legs more quickly, but it is also a good way to provide some dynamism to your stance. By keeping your knees 'soft' (that is, with slight movements up and down, never fully extending the knee joints and holding the legs completely straight) your body is in motion without your changing your weight distribution – this avoids your being completely static (which again makes subsequent horizontal movement that much slower, as well as providing an easier target) and helps to disconcert your opponent (*see* first sequence opposite).

Correct Weight Distribution

Standing in a sparring stance with feet flat …

… move your body forward until your rear heel just lifts off the floor …

… and then bend the rear knee, keeping the rear heel off the floor until you can feel the weight on the balls of your feet and you feel ready to move forward.

Keeping 'Soft' Knees

By keeping 'soft' knees you can raise and …

… drop your body by only an inch or two …

… to keep your body in motion, even when staying in the same spot.

Body Orientation

The final component of the sparring stance is the position of the rest of your body in relation to your legs and feet. If all the aspects above are correct then your trunk and hips should naturally face the same direction (slightly to the right, if your right leg is back and vice versa), presenting your body at an angle to your opponent. This position is the best compromise between a more full-facing position, as practised by boxers, that

Correct Body Orientation

The correct body orientation: head facing forwards and body at the same angle towards your opponent as your feet.

With the body too square you present a larger target for your opponent's kicks.

An overly defensive position shifts your body weight towards the rear foot.

21

is not well suited to defence against kicks and an even more defensive position where the hips are turned more towards the rear foot, which upsets your weight distribution. While the hips and the trunk are facing slightly away from your opponent, your head must face directly forward, giving you the best possible visibility (*see* second sequence on page 21).

Practice

As stated above, a good stance is fundamental to effective sparring and must become second nature to you when you fight. To achieve this is not easy since it requires not only much practice to be able to form the recommended stance at will, but even more practice to avoid falling back into more 'instinctive' habits. Clearly the stance

needs to be combined with correct movement and an effective guard. These are covered in the following chapters that contain drills for all these components; these will form the backbone of your practice regime. However, given the importance of the stance, it is always useful to return to basics and to concentrate solely on the stance and its components as detailed in this chapter, for which the following free-form drill is always useful (*see* sequence below).

You cannot practise to get the stance right often enough – in front of a mirror, as part of a warm-up, or even when waiting for the kettle to boil; every time that you snap into the stance adds another instance of the stance to your 'muscle memory' and makes it easier to maintain it when sparring, but note any shortcomings and try to rectify them the next time. Practice makes perfect.

Dynamic Stance Formation Drill

Starting with the body static in no particular stance ...

... drop straight into the basic sparring stance ...

... then jump slightly into the air while switching the legs ...

... to drop into the alternate side-facing stance.

4 Guard

Nobody likes being hit. A good stance and correct movement will help you to avoid attacks, but in Taekwon-Do or any other martial art with sparring that involves some contact, it is inevitable that you will be hit from time to time. For some people getting hit is a fleeting concern, they don't worry about it beforehand and forget about it afterwards; for others it is more of an issue and the fear of being hit can become more important than the actual blow. Maintaining and using a proper guard not only reduces the chances of an attack scoring against you but it also provides a strategy for coping with blows, thereby reducing your apprehension and increasing your self-confidence.

Again, as with the sparring stance, the demands of free sparring require us to look outside the formal syllabus of blocks and stances to find the optimum hand and body positions to stifle and absorb the range of kicks and punches that can be thrown.

Guard against What?

The primary purpose of the guard is to shield the most vulnerable targets from attack, which presents something of a problem given the variety of hand and foot techniques available and the different attacking ranges. The 'default' position is therefore determined by your defending against the attacks that you are most likely to face when you are in the sparring stance; these break down into three broad categories.

Turning Kicks

In Taekwon-Do sparring, the turning kick (also known as the roundhouse kick in other martial arts) is by far the most popular one, and it would be extremely rare to face an opponent who never used it. The reasons for its popularity provide useful pointers to an effective defence against it.

Ease of Execution

Most people find it relatively easy to execute a turning kick because it is a very 'forgiving' kick, where you can stray some distance from the technically 'correct' kick and still land an effective blow – the degree to which you chamber the leg, the angle of the foot on impact and the part of the foot used can all vary and it may still score a point. Because it is easy many fighters come to rely on it too much and throw little else – this creates a strategic opportunity for you, as will be discussed in the final section of the book.

Good Defensive Position

The attacker is in a good defensive position when delivering the turning kick: his body is out of range for a counter-punch and can be well protected with a guard in a half-facing position. Again, because people feel relatively secure throwing the turning kick it, they tend to prefer it to more 'exposing' techniques.

Versatility

Perhaps the most versatile of kicks, the turning kick can be thrown with the lead or rear leg and can be used against all areas of the body. If you have a fast and accurate turning kick and can master its variants, such as reverse turning kicks, jumping turning kicks and hooking kicks, then one core technique can deliver a wide range of attacks.

Power

Correctly executed, the turning kick gains a lot of momentum as it travels in an arc towards the target and can result in a powerful blow that is difficult to block in its later stages.

Surprise

Despite its popularity, the fact that it is delivered at an angle and therefore registers at the edge of your opponent's vision gives it the same character as a hook punch – if one's focus is drawn straight ahead the turning kick can be difficult to spot, even though it takes a relatively longer time to reach its target than a jab punch or a front snap kick.

From a defensive point of view, in a sparring stance you need to be able to deal with long (from your opponent's back leg) and middle-range (from the

Turning Kick Target Areas

Turning kick to the middle section on the open side (that is, the same side as the direction that the front of the body is facing).

Turning kick to the high section on the open side.

Turning kick to the high section on the closed side.

Piercing Kicks

The side kick and ...

... the back kick ...

... thrust the foot, heel first, into the abdomen.

front leg) turning kicks to three main target areas (*see* first sequence opposite).

Piercing Kicks

This category comprises powerful, thrusting, straight-line kicks, typically side kicks and back kicks (although it could be argued that front snap kicks target the same area in a straight line, they are less penetrating and their use in sparring is less frequent). In common with the turning kick, they can be performed with either the lead or the rear leg (in the case of the back kick this requires a 'switch' or rapid change of stance) and offer the attacker a similarly good defensive position, but they lack versatility since they are best and most commonly focused on the middle-section abdominal area. They present a particular challenge to Taekwon-Do fighters and other kicking martial artists that a boxer never has to deal with – a fast, direct and very powerful strike from long or middle range to the middle section. Difficult to block and to avoid, piercing kicks have the potential to be highly damaging (*see* second sequence opposite).

Short-Range Techniques

Both of the above categories encompass long- and middle-range kicking attacks but, as the distance between fighters shortens, there comes a point at which kicks cannot be thrown and your defensive priorities change. When fighters are too close to kick (although a few, exceptionally flexible fighters are able to execute kicks such as high-section hooking kicks or downward kicks at close range), their primary concern is with short-range hand techniques, the most common of which are shown below.

These shorter-range punches, back fist and other strikes are inherently faster than longer-range kicks and, although there may therefore be more thrown in a given length of time, they will generally lack the power of kicking techniques. From a defensive point of view they pose a different set of problems from the previous two categories of attacks: when at close range there are more, faster techniques thrown to a single target (high section) that will be harder to avoid but easier to intercept and absorb. Different guard strategies

Short-Range Techniques

The high-section jab.

The high-section hook.

The high-section back fist.

The middle-section reverse punch (or cross).

are therefore required for short- and for longer-range defences.

Basic Sparring Guard

Given the importance of kicks in Taekwon-Do and other martial arts, the way that this is reflected in the sparring scoring system and in fighters' natural enthusiasm for kicking, most fighters most of the time like to operate from within or just outside the kicking range (and, of course, within, or just outside the range for longer-range hand techniques such as stepping or jumping punches) and follow through into shorter punching range to pursue an attack. This pattern dictates that your initial and default defensive strategy is to deal with longer-range techniques to the high and the middle section and the basic sparring guard described here meets this requirement. Like the basic sparring stance, it has been modified from the standard boxing guard to cope with the

additional demands of defending against kicks and to incorporate current sparring trends. It is formed as shown below.

As with the basic sparring stance, the basic sparring guard needs to become your automatic, default position and you need to understand the 'why' as well as the 'how'; the principal components of the guard are examined in some detail next.

Stance

A correct stance is critical in adopting an effective guard for all of the reasons outlined in the previous chapter, but it is worth re-emphasizing that correct body positioning is a fundamental component of an effective guard.

When formed correctly, the basic sparring stance puts your body into the optimum defensive position and one that the basic guard can complement most effectively – if you deviate from this by turning your body too little or too

How to Form the Basic Sparring Guard

In the basic sparring stance, draw the rear hand up to about nose height, 2 or 3in from the face …

… to cover the jaw on the open side.

Bend the lead arm so that it protects the abdominal area and pull it across the body, raising the lead shoulder a little …

… to form the basic sparring guard.

much or through incorrect foot positioning you increase the opportunities for your opponent (*see* sequence below).

Also, on a more tactical level, when faced with a consistent and defensive body orientation your opponent will tend to limit his range of techniques to those that he thinks will be most effective, thereby making him easier to 'read'. This is an elementary example of 'training' your opponent – using your actions and behaviour to influence your opponent's and make it more predictable – which is a key component of effective sparring tactics that will be covered in the final section here. However, even at this fundamental level bear in mind that merely by maintaining a proper stance and guard you are presenting your opponent with a problem that will, to some extent, draw him into 'your' fight.

Lead-Arm Position

Your lead arm's primary purpose is to protect your body from kicks, and keeping it in the correct position is key to an effective defence against longer-range attacks to your middle section. The lead arm must deal with both frontal piercing kicks

Incorrect Body Orientation

Holding the body too squarely makes the middle section an easier target for piercing kicks ...

... and also increases the exposure of the closed-side chin.

Turning the body too much makes the floating ribs an attractive target for a shorter-range turning kick.

27

and angled turning kicks so the correct position is a compromise between these two demands, as is the manner in which it is held; while not held rigidly, which would make movement difficult, it must nonetheless be held sufficiently firmly to absorb frontal kicks with the shoulder slightly raised to offer some protection for the chin (*see* sequence below).

As stated, the basic guard needs to become your automatic default position and, if you make any changes to it, such as shown below when deflecting a turning kick, then you need to return to the correct guard position as soon as possible. Given the popularity of turning kicks, a common error is to fail to return the lead arm after deflecting or absorbing a turning kick, because, either consciously or unconsciously, you are anticipating further turning kick attacks, that is, you have been 'trained' to modify your guard. Faced with a strong, defensive guard, a more experienced fighter will often concentrate on one line of attack to create an opening for a different one and to focus on the front arm is a common tactic (*see* sequence opposite).

Correct Lead-Arm Position

With the lead arm in the correct position ...

... it is well placed to block piercing kicks and ...

... deflect turning kicks.

Importance of Returning to the Correct Lead-Arm Position

If you do not return your lead arm to the correct position after deflecting a kick ...

... you leave your middle section unprotected, allowing your opponent to continue his attack with ...

... a middle-section side kick.

Head Position

In contrast to the upright posture maintained in single-point sparring or forms of sparring where punching to the head is not permitted, the demands of contact sparring, where both high-section kicks and punches are permitted (and indeed, self-defence in the street) dictate that you *must* protect your chin at all times. While the rear arm has a key role to play, as detailed below, even more fundamental is how you hold your head, and, given the potential damage that a blow to the chin can cause, this is perhaps the single most important aspect of your defence. By dipping your chin towards your slightly raised shoulder with your head orientated straight towards your opponent, your chin is partially covered on your closed side, allowing you to drop it further into your shoulder as required.

As always, avoid too much tension in the neck or shoulder as this will inhibit your speed of movement (*see* first sequence on page 30).

Rear-Arm Position

The primary purpose of your rear arm in the basic sparring guard is to protect the side of your chin on your open side from longer-range kicks, yet it must also be able to adapt quickly to slightly higher kicks to the head or drop down to protect the middle section, as well as cope with the hand attacks to the head as the range between you and your opponent shortens. The optimum position to meet all of these requirements is to

Correct Head Position

... allows you to deflect the turning kick with your shoulder without having to change your guard.

Dipping the chin deeper into the lead shoulder ...

Correct Rear-Arm Position

... the elbow can be raised for the arm to protect the head from a high-section turning kick ...

With the rear arm in the correct position ...

... or dropped down to protect the body from a middle-section turning kick.

hold the arm with the fist facing outwards and the palm 2 to 3in from the upper jaw/cheekbone and with the elbow pointing straight downwards (*see* second sequence opposite).

Short-Range Guard

As previously stated, a different defensive strategy is required when fighters close the distance between them and move out of kicking range and into punching range. Again, we need to be adaptive and look outside the world of Asian martial arts and draw on the extensive and directly relevant experience on our own doorstep: that of Western boxing. The standard boxing guard is ideally suited to provide the best protection from short-range punches to both the head and the body and it is formed as shown in the sequence on page 32.

In moving from the basic sparring guard to the short-range guard you are removing the modifications to cater for longer-range attacks and reverting to the standard boxing guard by changing the position of the arms, not only so that they can defend against shorter-range attacks but also so that they can counter-attack as quickly as possible.

Lead-Arm Position

At close range the purpose of the lead arm is now threefold:

• to block/parry high-section hand attacks to the front and on the closed side
• to protect the ribs on the closed side
• to counter-attack

As always, the best position to achieve this is a compromise – in this case between a highly defensive position and too open an attacking one (*see* sequence on page 33).

With the lead arm held in the correct position you are best placed to carry out any of its three functions and to return as rapidly as possible to the short-guard position (*see* sequence on page 34).

Head Position

Although the position of the head has not changed from that in the basic sparring guard, it is important to note that, in changing the position of the lead arm, the lead shoulder has now dropped slightly to be in a better position to counter-attack with a jab or a hook punch and therefore offers less protection to the chin on the closed side. To drop the chin further would restrict your field of vision (which is even more important at short range) and you therefore need to be aware that, although you are in a better position to block high-section attacks and to counter-attack with the lead arm, the price that you will pay is that you are slightly more exposed on the closed side to angled techniques such as hook punches and you therefore need to be able draw the lead hand back rapidly to deal with them.

Rear-Arm Position

The purpose of the rear arm in the short-range guard mirrors that of the lead arm.

• to block/parry high-section hand attacks to the front and on the open side
• to protect the ribs on the open side
• to counter-attack

The only slight modification from the basic sparring guard is to hold the rear fist an inch or so lower to be in a better position to counter-attack with the cross (reverse) punch; again, the marginal increase in the exposure of the chin must be offset by increased vertical movement when required.

Keep Your Guard Up!

Being able to form a good, strong guard is one thing, but it is effective only when you use it – the single most important requirement is that you maintain your guard at all times, because without

How to Form the Short-Range Guard

In the basic sparring stance ...

... the rear hand is drawn up to the same height as for the standard guard but ...

... held more compactly to the body, 1 or 2in from the chin.

Then raise the lead hand to 1 or 2in below the chin ...

... with the arm bent at a right angle so that the lead hand is about 1½ft from the chin ...

... to form the short-range guard.

Incorrect Lead-Arm Positions

(a) If the arm is held too close in an extreme defensive position, such as completely covering up … (b) then, although the guard is good at absorbing blows … (c) it is not a good position from which to launch a counter-punch.

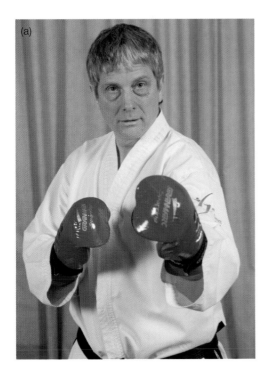

(a) A traditional karate guard … (b) is good for blocking a single punch in its early stages, but … (c) can be overwhelmed by multiple punches.

Correct Lead-Arm Position

With the lead hand in the correct position, it can easily parry punches with a small movement …

… as well as draw into the body to block hook punches …

… and always be at (or returning to) the correct height to counter-attack.

it you are completely exposed. Yet this seemingly obvious advice is actually hard to put into practice; why should this be? Largely for similar reasons why people find it initially difficult to maintain a good sparring stance, in that it is not something that is taught as part of the 'formal' syllabus and people tend to revert to what feels more 'natural' when under pressure. But, in addition to these underlying reasons, there are three specific situations where more inexperienced fighters tend to drop their guard.

1. Overreaction to an attack

Your basic instincts can sometimes work against you such as when you automatically raise your hands to fend off an attack, this is an overreaction that can make matters worse in a sparring situation (*see* sequence opposite).

This is a difficult reaction to control but it is one that you must because an experienced opponent will quickly spot and take advantage of it. Whatever defensive movements you make with your arms in response to an attack should be as small as possible so that you can get back behind your guard as quickly as possible.

2. Change of stance

When you move forward or backward and you change your foot position, you need to change your guard to match your stance (that is, arm on

Overreaction to an Attack

As the kick starts to come in …

… the defender raises both hands
to block the kick …

… exposing his middle section to a
rapid, consecutive side kick.

the same side as the rear leg protects the head, for example). (*See* sequence on page 36.)

Until fighters get used to synchronizing their guard and stance, it is surprising how common it is for them to 'forget' to change their guard, leaving them exposed to attack; try and think more 'defensively' and be more sensitive to errors in your guard.

3. Launching an attack

Once the decision to attack is made, less experienced fighters seem to switch out of the defence mode and completely abandon their guard – not only does this leave you exposed to a swift counter-attack but it also telegraphs the attack to your opponent, and, if you land with no guard after the kick, you are then left exposed to further counter-attacks (*see* first sequence on page 37).

Again, like overreaction to an attack, this appears to be an instinctive action that is difficult but necessary to control since a more experienced fighter will easily spot and exploit it. It is important to maintain your guard when attacking as well as when defending, as will be described in Chapter 6 and shown in all the attacking techniques throughout the rest of the book.

Change of Stance

As the defender steps back to avoid the turning kick …

… he 'forgets' to change his guard …

… leaving an opportunity for the attacker to score with a middle-section back kick.

While it is true that you may see more experienced fighters with no discernible guard, the chances are that this is part of their strategy to draw their opponent in (as discussed in the last section of the book) and, in any case, they will soon form a good guard when they need to. Such tactics are best left until you have complete confidence in your guard; for the present your constant reminder to yourself must be '*keep your guard up!*'

Practice

As with the stance, a good guard is absolutely fundamental to effective sparring and it must become almost instinctive to you when you fight. Every drill and exercise shown here will require you to maintain a basic sparring, short-range or modified (when attacking) guard so, along with the stance and correct movement,

Launching an Attack

The attacker's guard starts to drop as he kicks …

… leaving him completely unprotected as the kick is delivered and …

… therefore open to an easy counter-attack.

Dynamic Stance and Guard Formation Drill

From a starting position …

… snap into a standard sparring guard in one stance.

Then switch your stance and …

… snap into a short-range guard on the other side.

will always be at the heart of your sparring training. However, when warming up or in an idle moment it can usefully be combined with the free-form drill for stance formation, shown in the previous chapter (*see* sequence above).

Again, you cannot practise snapping into your default sparring stance and guard enough and it can always be improved – use a mirror to try to identify any weak spots and points for improvement. This is the foundation of your defence – practise hard to perfect it.

5 Movement

Watch good fighters from any martial arts background – Taekwon-Do, Muay Thai, karate or boxing – and note how they advance, retreat and avoid: their movements seem relaxed and assured, flowing yet explosive, economical and effective. Then contrast this with less experienced fighters and note how they seem more erratic, less decisive, busier yet less effective. What is the essential difference? The obvious answer is 'experience', but what lies beneath that? Why do some beginners seem to move better when sparring right from the start and why do some more experienced students still seem to be tripping over themselves? A fighter who moves well is confident, he knows where he wants to move to and he knows that he will get there quickly without giving his opponent any undue advantage. Experience will certainly improve your movement, but it must be built upon a fundamental understanding of what your goal is and how best to achieve it and this is the purpose of this chapter.

What the chapter does not attempt is to provide a comprehensive description of all the possible ways of stepping in any direction, with the attendant multitude of complicated foot-placement diagrams found in many martial arts manuals – they are frequently confusing, difficult to absorb and to put into practice. Rather, it seeks to build on the foundation of the basic sparring stance by establishing the fundamental principles for the best way of moving around the ring from the stance by looking in detail at two basic methods of movement: shuffling and side-stepping. These principles and movements are not restrictive in the sense that you must not deviate from them, but, in the same manner as the stance and guard described previously, they provide you with a deeper understanding of an aspect of sparring not generally covered in great depth in traditional martial arts classes. Once you have grasped these principles you can apply them to your wider range of movement and develop more effective strategies for closing distance when attacking and for increasing distance when defending.

Shuffling

Just as the basic sparring stance and guard need to become your default body position for sparring, your basic method of advancing and retreating needs to change from what it has probably been in the past – you need a new default method of forward and backward stepping to best complement your body position and that best suits the demands of Taekwon-Do sparring. And, once again, you need to go back to first principles to understand the need for yet another fundamental change to the way that you spar. In this case, the underlying objective that dictates the techniques that follow is simple: to allow you to advance and retreat as rapidly as possible, while compromising your guard and stance as little as possible. Unless you are attacking or defending you want to be in your default sparring position so that, when you are moving around the ring, your primary concern is to spend as little time as possible out of that position, because when your stance or guard is not fully implemented, your defence is weaker and you are at greater risk of attack. There are, of course, many ways in which your sparring stance and guard can be compromised when stepping, but there are three extremely common situations that must be avoided.

Changing Guard with a Full Stride

When the attacker is out of range and …

… closes in with a full step or stride …

… the defender can take advantage of the transition in the attacker's guard.

First, if your sparring is based on how basic techniques are taught in class, with full strides between each punch, kick or block going forwards and backwards (as is nearly always the case with beginners), then, even if you have a good guard, you are probably presenting your opponent with an ideal opportunity to attack (as shown above).

Secondly, in addition to the momentary opportunities presented to your opponent by frequent changes of guard when stepping with full strides, it is usually the case that an attacker coming forward with full strides is simply faster than a defender retreating in the same manner (*see* first sequence on page 40).

Finally, regardless of how you move, if you over-extend your stride you will find it harder to take the next step and therefore become a more static target (*see* second sequence on page 40).

While there will be situations where you will want or need to do the opposite, there are three general (that is, if there is no pressing reason to do otherwise) rules about stepping to be drawn from these situations:

- avoid changing your guard from side to side
- avoid crossing your legs
- avoid over-extending your stride.

These rules, combined with the use of the basic sparring stance and guard and the demands of Taekwon-Do sparring, have seen an alternative method of stepping come to the fore in recent years: sliding half-stepping or 'shuffling', as it is more straightforwardly known in Western boxing.

Forward Shuffling

You need to go forward when you are sparring; even if you are exceptionally good at avoiding attacks, you cannot rely solely on counter-attacking in continuous sparring and you must spend more time advancing than retreating. With your body weight on the balls of your feet and your rear leg primed to push off, the basic sparring stance puts you in the best possible position to move forward quickly, but, unlike a sprinter, you do not necessarily want to move as far as you can by taking a large stride, your main priority is to keep your guard in place and return to your stance as

Loss of Distance when Retreating with Full Strides

A determined advance by an attacker …

… will close the gap over multiple strides …

… and put the attacker in kicking range.

Danger of the Over-Extension of Stride

When an attacker over-extends his stride, such as when punching, …

… he will take even longer to shift his weight on to his back foot to stride backwards …

… giving the defender time to counter-attack.

soon as possible. All this can be achieved by using basic 'push-stepping' boxing footwork, where the front foot moves first, followed by the rear foot which 'catches up' with the front foot to re-form the boxing stance. This technique is fine at close quarters but is not best suited to the longer-range movement also required in Taekwon-Do sparring, as shown below.

The basic forwards shuffling technique presented here maintains the defensive attributes of the boxing movement but covers a greater distance and provides increased manoeuvrability to cater for the demands of middle- and long-range kicks (*see* sequence on page 42).

As with the basic sparring stance and guard, this method of stepping will feel somewhat unnatural as you start to practise it and your body will try to revert to your normal pattern of movement. Again, this needs to become your new default method of stepping and constant practice of this basic technique is required to absorb it into your 'muscle memory'. Incorporate it (and the backward shuffling described below) into your warm-up routine, practise in front of a mirror at every opportunity to link all three fundamental components – stance, guard and step – together so that they all flow from and into each other. And as you start to become more familiar with it, you can start to build upon it and extend its use into two important areas.

First, since the distance travelled is controlled by the power you use to push off from the rear leg, you have much greater flexibility than that

Limitation of Push-Stepping

Moving the front foot first ...

... limits the size of the step that you can take, making you ...

... more susceptible to a kick before you are in punching range.

Basic Forward Shuffling

From a basic sparring stance …

… the rear foot starts to push off and …

… draws close to the front foot, maintaining a shoulder's width between the feet as …

… the front foot moves forward to reform the sparring stance.

Forward shuffling allows the attacker to …

… maintain his guard while still …

… covering a full stride's distance.

provided by either push-stepping or striding, as shown below.

With practice, you will find that you can cover a substantial distance with a single step, perhaps double that which you would cover with two 'normal' steps. This increased flexibility of the distance covered with the same movement makes your intentions harder to read and consequently it is easier for you to surprise your opponent – a simple drill can help to extend distance and develop timing (*see* first sequence on page 44).

Second, as well as varying the distance within the same movement, you can vary the angle at which you travel 'late' in the stepping movement, since the decision as to whether to travel in a straight line or on a diagonal need not be made until after the rear foot has moved. Once you have become proficient in the technique you will be much better able to position yourself quickly towards your opponent's side to pursue your attack, as in this example (*see* second sequence on page 44).

Increasing Range when Forward Stepping

To cover a greater distance when forward shuffling, push off strongly with the rear leg …

… and allow the lead leg to travel freely forward as far as it can, then …

… draw the rear leg back up into sparring stance, moving the front foot further forward as necessary.

Drill for Increasing Range with Reverse Punch

From outside the punching range …

… try and score with an extended shuffle and a single-hand technique and …

… then back off immediately.

Moving Diagonally When Forward Shuffling

The attacker starts to push off from rear foot and …

… pivots diagonally as his rear foot lands, sending him to the side of his opponent and in a good position to …

… deliver a lead-leg turning kick.

Backward Shuffling

Before we consider the differences in technique for retreating, there is a crucial one to advancing to bear in mind and it is one of psychology. When you are retreating from your opponent's attacks you are reacting under some pressure and you are in a different frame of mind than when you are actively pursuing your attacking strategy. As your subconscious imperative for self-preservation comes to the fore and your adrenalin levels rise, enabling you to move faster, your mind inevitably becomes more focused on the task in hand rather than on your next attacking opportunity. Yet this is where the counter-attack is most effective – when your opponent thinks he has you on the run. Experience and training help you to retain your focus when under pressure and to recognize the better opportunities for counter-attacking, but there is an aspect of stepping backwards that, if you concentrate on it from the beginning, will help you to become a much more effective counter-attacker: reverting to the proper stance and not 'falling' backwards. And this is the great advantage of the following method of backward shuffling: after each step you are always ready to advance.

When backward shuffling all of the same considerations as for forward stepping apply – the need to keep your guard up, to revert to your stance quickly, to cover variable distances and to change direction diagonally – therefore the same basic technique is applied, but in reverse (*see* page 46).

Similarly, the reverse of the techniques for increasing range and moving diagonally when stepping forwards can be applied when stepping backwards (*see* page 47).

A Final Point

While some of the many advantages of shuffling, as opposed to other forms of stepping, have been outlined above, there is one final point to be made about (perhaps the most important advantage of) employing this method of stepping: *it keeps you on the balls of your feet.*

Look at the good fighters in the next competition you attend – look at their feet: how often are they flat-footed? What happens when they are? If a fighter is flat-footed and his heels are on the floor then it will always take him longer to move in any direction simply because his body is not 'ready' to move. Think about your own sparring. If, like most club fighters, you have your good times when everything seems to 'flow' and your bad times when you seem leaden and keep getting caught, the chances are that when things are going well you are more on the balls of your feet and moving faster.

There are no secrets to improving your sparring, but this simple point comes close: every aspect of your sparring will improve if your body is ready to move. The discipline of maintaining your correct sparring stance and stepping by using this technique forces you to keep your weight on the balls of your feet which, in turn, increases your speed and range of movement.

Side-Stepping

Good lateral movement is an absolute necessity for effective sparring and yet, along with being flat-footed, having little or no lateral movement is one of the commonest failings of less experienced fighters. As with movement in general, much is determined by how martial arts classes are traditionally taught, with striding movements up and down the hall focusing on techniques rather than 'ring craft'. And, as with all the topics that have been covered here so far, you need to recognize the limitations of what you have been doing and make yourself open to alternative approaches that may, at first, seem awkward. This is particularly the case with side-stepping: most club-level fighters lapse into a familiar pattern when sparring, where the bout becomes a series of advances and retreats along a straight line and may often seem more like a pre-arranged sparring exercise (where each fighter carries out an agreed number of attacks before the other counter-attacks and the roles reverse) than free sparring. We hope

Basic Backward Shuffling

From a basic sparring stance …

… the front foot starts to push off …

… and draws close to the rear foot, maintaining a shoulder's width between the feet and …

… the rear foot moves backwards to re-form the sparring stance.

As the attacker starts to step forward, the defender starts to push off …

… maintaining his guard as the front foot moves back …

… into the sparring stance.

Increasing Range when Backward Shuffling

As the attacker moves in with a step, the defender starts to move his front foot back ...

... and then pushes back forcefully ...

... sliding back into the sparring stance.

Moving Diagonally when Backward Shuffling

After moving the front foot back ...

... pivot diagonally on the front foot and ...

... push back into the sparring stance.

you can now recognize that an underlying reason for this pattern is that, in the absence of a good sparring stance, the fighters have little option but to stride backwards and forwards since they are not well prepared to move in any other way. If you can combine effective side-stepping with the linear and diagonal shuffling outlined above, you will be able to break out of this pattern, which, in turn, will allow you to defend better, create more openings for attack and, crucially, be less predictable.

Basic Side-Stepping

For basic side-stepping (that is, moving at 90 degrees to the direction that you are facing), the most straightforward technique that best preserves the stance and guard is that practised in Western boxing, where the foot closer to the desired direction of travel moves first and the other follows (*see* first sequence opposite).

When moving to your open side, the procedure is simply reversed (*see* second sequence opposite).

This basic movement is most effective when you want to take a single, relatively small step to the side to avoid (typically) a straight-line, middle- or long-distance attack. If you are not used to it, then stepping to the side to avoid attacks can seem quite daunting when your 'natural' reaction is to retreat, but it is well worth persevering with since it can put you in an excellent position to counter-attack (*see* first sequence on page 50).

Equally, a quick step to the side can be highly effective in getting around your opponent's guard (*see* second sequence on page 50).

As you incorporate these quick, single steps into your sparring you will not only recognize their effectiveness but also their limitations, the principal one being that you are limited in the distance that you can travel both in a single step (since you do not want to over-extend your stride) and in the relative slowness in putting multiple steps together (since you are not making use of the explosive power of your legs as when you are shuffling). What is therefore required is a way of incorporating shuffling with a step to the side.

Splitting to the Side

If you want to cover more ground when moving to the side of your opponent then you need to be in the correct stance to shuffle in that direction (facing the direction that you want to travel) and the fastest way to achieve that is to change stance and direction in a single motion, generally known as 'splitting' (*see* page 51).

While it is possible to split to the closed side, you must change your guard around and you will find it hard in practice to move sideways relative to your opponent – generally it is better merely to switch stance before you split (*see* first sequence on page 52).

In either case, the distance travelled can be greatly increased by adding a shuffle to the technique that can better position you to deliver a longer-range counter-attack (*see* second sequence on page 52).

Of all the fundamental sparring movements that the authors teach, this simple technique is one of the hardest for students to grasp. There are two major reasons for this: first, although the technique is not difficult in itself, it exposes any weaknesses in your stance or stepping and, secondly, like much that has been introduced so far, it is not a 'natural' response under pressure, where your instinct is to take a large stride in the opposite direction from which an attack is coming – moving sideways is not instinctive, splitting and shuffling even less so. And yet these difficulties highlight the very reasons why you should perfect this technique. Being able to split quickly and fluidly to the side and shuffle off is a final confirmation that your stance and basic movement are correct; if you can execute this technique at will then your movement will be superior to that of most club-level martial artists. But perhaps even more importantly, this technique combined with the shuffling lifts you out of the straight-line, sparring 'routine', allowing you to be more confident, more creative and therefore more effective in your sparring. However, constant repetition is required to perfect the technique

Basic Side-Stepping to the Closed Side

From the sparring stance ...

... move your front foot half a shoulder width to your closed side ...

... then move your rear foot across and into the sparring stance.

Basic Side-Stepping to the Open Side

From the sparring stance ...

... move your rear foot half a shoulder width to your open side ...

... then move your front foot across and into the sparring stance.

sufficiently to reap these benefits and you cannot perform the drill shown on page 53 often enough.

Practice

With the fundamentals of stance, guard and movement in place, they can all be incorporated into a single practice regime to improve your movement around the ring – but with major changes in all of these areas, this will require considerable practice. Once a basic proficiency has been achieved in all three elements, the next (and far harder) task is to make the techniques more natural to you in the sense that they have a familiarity and do not require to be thought about before you execute

Side-Stepping to Avoid a Side Kick

As the attacker starts to kick, the defender side-steps …

… leaning away as the kick is completed before …

… counter-attacking with a rear-leg turning kick.

Side-Stepping to Launch a Side Kick

The attacker steps to the side with the rear foot and …

… chambers the front leg immediately to …

… deliver a high-section side kick.

50

Splitting to the Open Side

From a sparring stance …

… pivot on both feet so that your body is turned towards your open side …

… then, almost simultaneously, push off on the rear foot and let the lead foot travel forwards …

… bringing the rear foot forward into the sparring stance.

As soon as the attacker starts to kick …

… the defender splits to the side …

… and completes a turn of his body just in time to avoid the side kick.

them. There is a lot to take in here – maintaining your stance and guard, shuffling, side-stepping, splitting and stance switching – and it is going to take many repetitions before these techniques become your norm. One approach would be to practise individual techniques assiduously (for example, 'split to the right twice, split to the left twice and repeat fifty times'). But, not only is this boring, it also fails to give you any sense of context and rhythm; you need to develop a feel for when one type of movement can practically and effectively follow another, while at the same time being inventive and unpredictable in how you move around the ring. The best way to

Switching Stance to Split to the Closed Side

From the sparring stance … … switch the stance … … rapidly … … and split to your (now) open side as soon as you land in the new stance.

Splitting to the Side and Shuffling

After splitting to the side … … an additional shuffle can position you well to the side of your opponent … … to attack with a long-range technique such as the reverse turning kick.

achieve these goals is to practise set routines of increasing complexity and to approach them in much the same way as you would in learning ballroom dancing, that is, not just learning the moves but also developing rhythm.

This is a difficult concept to impart in a book, but the analogy with dancing is a useful one: when you start to learn to dance your movements are jerky and uncertain and you spend more time looking at your feet than your partner.

Drill for Splitting to the Side

From the sparring stance … … split to your open side … … and shuffle one step … … forward.

Then snap into the opposite stance to your starting stance … … split to your open side … … shuffle forward one step … … and finally snap back into the stance you started in, ready to repeat.

At first, progress might be quite slow as you learn the basic steps and their sequence in the dance, but, once you have grasped this, things speed up as your movements seem to 'fit' the music more and you develop your sense of rhythm – you can sense when it is right (or at least better) when it flows together and is not laboured. Once you have reached the stage where you have learned a single dance and have a sense of how it should feel performing it, you will then find it easier to learn other dances. And so it is with sparring movement practice: start off with a relatively simple routine, practise it until it flows and you are no longer concentrating on what comes next, speed it up so that you can perform it in a fairly rapid rhythm and then move on to more complex routines. However, where the analogy with ballroom dancing breaks down is that your ultimate goal is not to learn a series of predetermined steps but to be able to link together and execute new combinations of steps as the situation demands. So, rather than list numerous practice routines, the process by which a routine is developed is described here in detail to enable you to create your own movement practice drills and thereby encourage you to think more deeply about and be more inventive in your movement around the ring.

A good starting point is to take a relatively simple situation (perhaps one that you tend to perform badly in or that you tend to avoid) such as retreating, moving to the side and counterattacking – a useful skill when you are forced back to the edge of the ring – and to work out a series of steps, as shown below.

You now have a basic drill that incorporates shuffling and splitting that you can practise on your own, perfecting your footwork. As your footwork improves and flows more smoothly, you can focus more on visualizing your opponent and introduce some sparring techniques (*see* first sequence opposite).

With the core drill now in place, it only remains to make it 'continuous' – to be able to perform it in both directions without moving up or down the training area after each repetition. Since you are now on the same horizontal line but in the opposite stance, all you have to do is repeat the routine in the opposite direction (*see* second sequence opposite).

Once you have mastered the drill to the point where you can practise it continuously, you can introduce a further level of complexity and realism by practising it with a partner (*see* sequence on page 56).

Basic Stepping for Drill

From the sparring stance shuffle back one step ...

... split to your open side ...

... shuffle one step forward ...

... turn and face your starting direction.

Introducing Sparring Techniques to the Drill

From the sparring stance …

… shuffle back and block a high-section turning kick on your open side …

… split to your open side, blocking a side kick and …

… shuffle one step forward.

Next turn and face and …

… attack with a rear-leg turning kick …

… retract leg and step down into …

… the sparring stance.

Making the Drill Continuous

From the sparring stance after the rear-leg turning kick …

… split to your open side, blocking side kick …

… shuffle one step forward …

… and snap back into your starting stance and position.

Full Drill with Partner

The defender shuffles back to block a rear-leg turning kick …

… then splits to the side to avoid and block a side kick.

After both have shuffled, turned and faced each other, the defender counters with a turning kick and …

… the attacker replies with a side kick that the defender avoids and blocks by splitting to the side.

Both shuffle back to the start and …

… snap back into their starting stances and positions.

As you get more used to the drill you can vary it as you choose – such as introducing more steps, different attacks and counter-attacks – but remember that the footwork is your primary concern. Try and focus on maintaining a rhythm and a consistency to your movements, make the drill flow without stopping and make sure that each step is of the same length so that you always end up where you started as you begin another cycle. Above all, don't get bored. If you are a typical club-level martial artist then you probably need to practise movement more than any aspect of your sparring and you will need to spend much time doing so and refining your drills. Set yourself challenges to make them more interesting, even if they may not be directly relevant to what you actually do in sparring; for instance, switching stance twice after each step or jumping and turning a full 360 degrees before landing; the more you practise movement outside your 'comfort zone', the better your movement inside the ring will become and the more your sparring will improve. But it takes a lot of practice.

6 Defence

A good defence is absolutely fundamental to effective Taekwon-Do sparring. When you step out into the ring or on to the mat, you are (and if you aren't, you should be) making a statement that you have confidence in your ability to defend yourself; if you don't, then you are going to be intimidated from the start and you will most likely be defeated. You must accept that your opponent is going to try and hit you: sometimes you will be able to avoid his attacks, sometimes you will block and absorb them and sometimes he will score, but you must always try to protect yourself to the best of your ability at all times, including when you are attacking. Your defence is not therefore limited to merely trying to neutralize your opponent's attacks, it must underpin all aspects of your sparring – not only in how you fight physically but also in your attitude towards your opponent. If you have that confidence that your opponent is going to have to work hard to get through your defence, that he is unlikely to hurt you if he does and that, even if he lands a good shot, it is not going to unnerve you, then you have a good defence.

And that is the purpose of this chapter: to develop your confidence in the defence that you have largely already built with your sparring stance, guard and movement by putting it into practice in defending against common attacks. As with the previous chapter, it does not attempt to cover every possible defensive move but to get you performing and developing effective drills for the most common situations to build up your defensive skills and to make them more instinctive. But the drills serve another crucial purpose: to get you used to being hit and to develop confidence in your ability to absorb kicks and punches and be ready physically and mentally to counter-attack strongly.

Sparring Drills

Before going on to detail the defensive sparring drills, there are a few points to be made about sparring drills in general and their importance here. There are many ways to practise different aspects of sparring, all of which have their merits, however, most of the practice drills in this chapter and the rest of this book are 'sparring drills' that try to emulate actual sparring conditions. The reason for this is that the authors take the view that this is the most effective way to make the techniques practised become more 'instinctive', while, at the same time, constantly reinforcing the fundamentals of stance, guard and movement – it is only by trying to hit someone on the actual target that you will develop correct distance and timing and it is only by facing reasonably strong blows to the target area that you can test and develop your defence. Therefore under this training system the sparring gloves serve as the target by either protecting the defender's target area or acting as a target in their own right (*see* sequence on page 58).

In addition, all of the sparring drills here share the following characteristics.

Use of Sparring Gear

Foot protectors and sparring gloves must always be worn, not only to protect the defender but also the attacker's hands and feet; further, by training in your sparring equipment you become more

Use of Gloves in Sparring Drills

Using the gloves and forearms to fully protect the head from a turning kick.

Holding the arms firmly crossed just in front of the stomach provides an absorbing target for piercing kicks.

Crossing the gloves above the head makes a good stretch target for jumping punches.

used to it and the level of protection that it offers. Depending on your preference, groin, mouth, shin and head guards may also be worn but these should not be necessary from a safety point of view when performing pre-arranged drills.

Drilling with a Partner

While there may well be benefit in practising sparring techniques on your own (as when focusing on your footwork or developing power by using a heavy punch bag), there is no substitute for training with a partner, ideally of a similar size and level of ability to yourself, who can move unpredictably and, above all, hit back. Nothing else can better simulate actual sparring

conditions or provide the vital experience of blocking and absorbing attacks; it is also more fun and more motivating to train and make progress with others.

One for One

When training with a partner, try and perform the drills on a 'one for one' basis where you attack and your partner defends and you then swap roles for the next repetition. This helps you to keep your techniques crisp, whereas multiple consecutive repetitions can lead to your losing interest, and it also helps you to examine your techniques more broadly by continually changing between attack and defence.

Change Stance

You must make sure that you practise the drills equally in both fighting stances (that is, with the left leg forward and then the right leg forward). Initially you may agree with your partner to do a certain number in one stance and then switch to the other, but as you become more familiar with a particular drill you can make it more challenging by allowing the attacker to choose which stance to use. To make it yet more challenging (and more realistic), you can incorporate a degree of feinting before attacking.

Continuous Motion

If you are static when you are sparring then you are an easier target and you will be slower off the mark when you want to move, so it is most important that you get into the habit of moving continuously when performing sparring drills – at no time, including when waiting for the next repetition of the drill, should you be static. Minimally, there should be some knee flexion in your stance, as described in Chapter 3, and you can complement this with upper-body movement or feinting as described in subsequent chapters, as well as a limited amount of additional stepping as the particular drill and the amount of space available allow.

Reasonable Contact

A major benefit of these drills is that they give you experience in hitting on target and of being hit, so it is important that they are practised with vigour and realism. Both defender and attacker know what is coming, so techniques should be delivered with sufficient accuracy, speed and power that the attacker would score if the defender took no action and that the defender actually 'needs' to defend himself. Clearly, making every technique full-on could result in injury and you need to find a compromise between this and a level of realism that both training partners are comfortable with. However, at all costs, you must avoid merely going through the motions with half-hearted techniques that will not only teach you

nothing but may even give you a false (and potentially dangerous) sense of confidence when sparring with unfamiliar fighters.

Intensity

As well as developing sparring skills, sparring drills should also be viewed as physical training routines and they should be practised frequently, vigorously and for extended periods.

A final and crucial point about sparring drills: put them into practice. Always remember that the purpose of your training is to improve your sparring and this will happen only if you make a conscious effort to use the techniques learnt in your training when you are actually fighting. Most fighters, both beginners and the more experienced, tend to rely on what they are most comfortable with and they can find it difficult to introduce new techniques when under pressure, but this is exactly the time at which to try something new. While not every technique in the book will necessarily work for you, you will never know if you do not give it a chance – the more you practise realistically, the easier it will be to draw on what you have learnt and incorporate new techniques and strategies into your sparring.

Long-Range Defence

As your opponent comes within attacking range, your initial and primary defensive concern is kicks and, as with all attacks, you have two choices: to stand your ground and block/absorb the kick or to evade it. While it is always exciting to watch a good evasive fighter who has good ring craft and counter-attacking skills, this is far from the norm. For most club-level fighters 'evasion' usually means 'retreat' by stepping back out of range and this is therefore not a strategy that can be maintained since you will soon run out of ring. Certainly there is a place for evasion and this will be covered later, but, as a general strategy, it is far better to stand your ground and neutralize your opponent's kick – frustrating him and providing you with a good opportunity to counter-attack.

Consequently, most of what follows covers some key techniques for blocking and absorbing kicks, followed by some effective alternatives to merely stepping backwards.

Blocking Turning Kicks

As stated earlier, the turning kick is the most popular and most versatile one in Taekwon-Do sparring, providing three separate target areas to defend.

Blocking High-Section Turning Kicks to the Open Side

An opponent with good flexibility will usually try to use it to get the extra point available by kicking to the head and that will normally involve a turning kick to your (assuming that you are in a well-formed, side-facing guard) high section on your open side (your right side if your body is turned towards the right). Fortunately, with the correct guard, your rear hand and forearm are

Blocking High-Section Turning Kicks to the Open Side

As the attacker starts to kick …

… turn your upper body into the kick slightly while raising the rear hand to cover the temple and …

… continue turning into the kick at the point of impact – bringing the lead arm across the body can brace the blocking arm and provide further protection.

Drill for Blocking a High-Section Turning Kick to the Open Side

With the attacker in motion and …

… the defender maintaining his position and distance …

… the attacker kicks at will and the defender must block.

already in the optimum position to absorb the kick with minimal movement (*see* first sequence opposite).

By getting behind your rear hand and bracing yourself into the kick, you will not only be able to block the kick effectively but you will also show your opponent that you are not going to be easily intimidated by standing your ground and shrugging off what can be a powerful technique if executed with the rear leg. Practise this basic block

with your partner to perfect your timing so that you tense your arm to absorb the kick at just the right time (*see* second sequence opposite).

The block is not only effective against the turning kick but also against any other kick targeting the high section on the open side that takes a similar trajectory, and you can incorporate these into the drills (*see* first sequence below).

As you practise the block, you will start to appreciate that you can absorb quite powerful

Blocking Other Angled High-Section Kicks to the Open Side

Reverse turning kick.

Hooking kick.

Jumping reverse turning kick.

Blocking and Counter-Attacking a High-Section Turning Kick to the Open Side

As the attacker starts to kick …

… move into the kick and block it further up the leg, which …

… puts you in range to counter with a strong, high-section cross.

Drill for Blocking Multiple High-Section Kicks to the Open Side

One fighter attacks with a high-section, reverse turning kick to the open side …

… then both fighters are in motion until …

… the other fighter responds with his choice of high-section kick to the open side.

kicks without injury and your confidence in your guard will increase, allowing you to relax more when sparring, which will, in turn, help you to anticipate better and react faster. If you can anticipate your opponent's kick and step in to meet his attack then this block can put you in an excellent position for a fast counter-attack (*see* second sequence on page 61).

To test your blocking and improve your timing more, incorporate all of the above in a single, 'semi-free' sparring drill (*see* sequence above).

Blocking Middle-Section Turning Kicks to the Open Side

When you are in a good sparring stance, the only readily available middle-section target is on your open side and you need to be able to block such attacks without compromising your high-section defence (a common tactic being to kick to the middle section to get the defender to drop his guard and expose his head to a rapid, second, high-section turning kick). If the kick is delivered with less power (particularly from your opponent's

Using the Lead Arm to Block Middle-Section Turning Kick to the Open Side

As the attacker starts to kick with his lead leg …

… and defender slightly turns his body into the kick …

… to block the kick with his lead arm.

lead leg) and is coming towards the front of your body, then you may have an opportunity to block the kick with your lead arm (*see* second sequence opposite).

The risks of using the lead arm to block middle-section, angled kicks to the open side are that you move your arm across your body too much, creating an opening for a piercing kick, and that it may not be strong enough to block a powerful rear-leg kick – if in doubt, the safest option is to block the kick by using the rear arm (*see* first sequence below).

In practice, unless your opponent is clearly only just within kicking range, it is difficult to judge where a middle-section turning kick is going to land, and your most effective block is going to be a combination of both techniques, that is, a slight movement of the arm across the body while dipping the body into the kick and slightly lowering the rear hand. While you can put together

Using the Rear Arm to Block a Middle-Section Turning Kick to the Open Side

As the attacker starts to kick with his rear leg …

… the defender turns into the kick …

… dropping his rear elbow to block it with his rear arm.

Drill for Blocking High- and Middle-Section Kicks to the Open Side

One fighter starts to kick and …

… opts for a middle-section turning kick to the open side then …

… the other replies with, for instance, a high-section, reverse turning kick.

Drill for Blocking Consecutive, Middle- and High-Section Kicks to the Open Side

One fighter attacks with a middle-section turning kick to the open side and …

… follows up with a consecutive high-section kick, then …

… the other fighter responds with a high-section, reverse turning kick followed by … etc.

a simple drill to practise blocks for kicks to the middle section, all the variations of angled kicks to the open side can now be pulled together in a single sparring drill that forces you to keep the blocking movements small in order to handle any angled kick to the open side (*see* second sequence on page 63).

A final variation on this drill, which further trains you to keep movements small and not to create any openings when blocking kicks to your open side, is to use a 'double' turning kick, where the initial kick is followed rapidly by a second one to an alternate target without fully re-chambering the leg (*see* sequence above).

Blocking and Counter-Attacking a High-Section Turning Kick to the Closed Side

As the attacker starts a turning kick to defender's closed side, shoulder starts to come up and …

… defender turns into the kick with his head well tucked in and …

… is in a good position to counter with a high-section, cross punch …

Blocking High-Section Turning Kicks to the Closed Side

Again, a correct sparring stance, where your body is angled away from your opponent, restricts his opportunity for turning kicks on your closed side to a single target: your head. Given the accuracy and flexibility that these techniques require, they tend to be used by more experienced fighters who will typically throw them after several attacks to the open side to increase the element of surprise (particularly by using a reverse turning kick). This presents a difficulty from a defensive point of view in that your rear arm cannot protect your head on the closed side and your lead arm should (in most circumstances) remain in place to protect your body on the open side and from middle-section piercing kicks, making your best general defensive option to try and avoid rather block them. Although it is possible to reverse your guard and take the kick on your lead arm, this should not be necessary if your chin is well tucked in and your shoulder sufficiently raised (*see* second sequence opposite).

Although not without risk, if executed correctly this defence can be very disquieting for your opponent, as you effectively shrug off his attack – the key to success is being able to anticipate the technique and to time your defence to best neutralize his attack.

Blocking Piercing Kicks

Although not quite as popular as turning kicks, the speed and penetration of piercing kicks, such as the side kick, make them potentially highly damaging and, if you can't avoid them, then a correct guard and stance are essential to defend against them. In practice, straight-line kicks are rarely thrown to the high section in Taekwon-Do sparring because they are faster, more powerful and therefore more effective when targeting the middle section and this is your primary defensive concern. Body position is key here – the more 'square' you are, the larger the target area and the greater the opportunity for the piercing kick (*see* first sequence on page 66).

By restricting the available target area with correct positioning, your lead arm can now fully protect your middle section, allowing you to absorb the piercing kick on the arm, while slightly dipping the body into the kick to increase the dampening effect (*see* second sequence on page 66).

However, you must be aware of the greater penetration of the piercing kick over the turning kick and brace your arms and body strongly at the point of impact – timing is key here and the following drill will help you develop this and get you used to facing up to the power of piercing kicks (*see* third sequence on page 66).

Evading Kicks

The natural tendency to retreat by striding backwards in the face of an attack and the resulting problems such as loss of balance and changing the guard have already been described and this tendency is strongest when under pressure from your opponent's kicking due to the distance covered and the potential force of the blow. Most fighters will exploit this tendency by launching a series of kicks to close the distance, weaken the defence and try to score with the final technique – indeed, many bouts of sparring seem to consist of little other than alternating flurries of kicks, as one side advances and the other retreats and vice versa. Breaking this rhythm disquiets your opponent, creating much better scoring opportunities for you – evading kicks with footwork and body movement provides another method of achieving this, alongside standing your ground and blocking. But there is a crucial consideration to be made when stepping out of range of a kick (or a long-distance hand technique, such as a stepping punch): when you are standing your ground, your guard allows you to react rapidly to your opponent's kicks both before and after they have been thrown – unless you are moving well out of range, you need to anticipate your opponent's technique before you move or you run the risk of moving on to his kick.

Correct Body Position Restricting the Target Area for Middle-Section Piercing Kick

It you are too square then …

… you present an easy target for a side kick, but …

… a more sideways body orientation presents a smaller target and makes it much easier to avoid the kick.

Using Standard Guard to Block Middle-Section Piercing Kick

As the defender sees the kick start, he drops his rear arm slightly and moves his lead arm across his body until …

… both arms are held tightly together a couple of inches from the body and …

… the body leans slightly into the kick to best absorb the impact.

Drill for Blocking Middle-Section Piercing Kick

The defender sees a kick starting and prepares to absorb …

… a back kick and then responds with, …

… for instance, a side kick.

Much of the ground for evading kicks with footwork has already been covered previously with the various methods of stepping in different directions, maintaining your guard and stance and therefore being ready to counter-attack immediately – in the same way as you need to develop your own practice drills for movement, you have the tools to develop your own evasion drills and techniques. Presented below are two additional core evasion techniques for specific situations that you can analyse, practise and then build on and incorporate into your own sparring strategies.

Moving out of Range

While standing your ground is a good base strategy, sometimes, when, for instance, you are under a lot of pressure or you are unable to read your opponent's kick, you have to get as far out of range as quickly as you can and the simplest way to do this is to step backwards. A slight modification to the step to turn it into more of a pivot allows you to move faster and be better prepared to counter-attack (*see* sequence below).

By deliberately keeping your weight forward and not falling, you can quickly put a full stride's distance between you and your opponent, such that you are taking a new 'stand' rather than embarking on a longer retreat. If your opponent likes to come forward with consecutive rear-leg kicks and is expecting you to continue travelling backwards, then this simple technique can be highly effective in drawing your opponent on to your counter-attack (*see* first sequence on page 68).

Alternatively, pivoting backwards and looking well prepared to advance may cause your opponent momentarily to pause his advance, still giving you an opportunity to counter but this time from a longer range (*see* second sequence on page 68).

Another useful technique for when you want to get out of range rather than merely avoid a kick is to split to the side, as described in the previous chapter. This technique is particularly effective against 'readable' high-section kicks to

Pivoting Backwards

As the defender starts to move his lead foot back ...

... he keeps his weight forward, pivoting on the ball of his rear foot ...

... avoiding the attack and being well placed to counter.

Pivoting Backwards and Counter-Attacking at Medium Range

The defender pivots to avoid the first turning kick, ...

... the attacker starts the second kick, expecting the defender to continue to retreat but ...

... the defender rapidly counters with a high-section cross.

Pivoting Backwards and Counter-Attacking at Long Range

After the defender has pivoted out of range, the attacker hesitates in his advance and ...

... the defender counters with ...

... a back kick.

your closed side, such as rear-leg turning kicks or reverse turning kicks – although more difficult to perform than pivoting backwards, it has the advantage that it puts you in the perfect position to counter-attack (*see* first sequence opposite.)

Avoidance

To avoid an opponent's kick while still remaining within his kicking range not only requires good footwork and body movement but also foresight – you need to have a reasonable idea of what kind of attack is coming. While you cannot read your

Splitting to the Side and Counter-Attacking

As the attacker kicks …

… the defender splits to his open side and is …

… well placed to deliver a rear-leg counter.

opponent's mind, you can build up a surprisingly accurate picture of how he spars in a relatively short space of time, and you can further 'influence' him in his choice of attack by presenting a target or 'training' him, as discussed in the final section of the book. For the present, if you can anticipate a straight-line attack, such as a side kick or a back kick (or even a stepping punch), then the easiest way to avoid the kick and still stay in close counter-attacking range is to pivot to the side (*see* sequence below).

While the advantage of this technique is that it places you in an excellent position to counter-attack and your opponent in a poor position to launch a follow-up attack, it has an obvious disadvantage in that if you misjudge the kick then you could end by walking into a turning kick launched against your closed side. When you see your

Pivoting to the Closed Side

As the defender registers the attacker's side kick, he …

… pivots on his front foot to his closed side to avoid the kick and …

… counter with a high-section cross.

Pivoting to the Open Side

As the attacker kicks …

… the defender pivots on his front foot to his open side and …

… counters with a jumping punch.

opponent start a kick with his leg on your closed side and you want to hedge your bets between an angled kick and a piercing kick then an alternative to splitting to your open side is to pivot there instead (*see* sequence above).

If you can read your opponent well and you have fast enough reactions then pivoting to the side and delivering a fast, close-range counterpunch can not only score a point but also dent your opponent's confidence as he sees that you have anticipated his attack and that you have not even needed to block it or to retreat out of range. However, you must use the technique selectively since it carries the risk of your misreading your opponent's attack and actually walking on to it, and, in the case of pivoting to your open side, leaving you exposed at close range: wait until you can see a pattern to your opponent's attack and get in fast with your counter.

Short-Range Defence

As the distance between fighters closes and shorter-range punches become the defensive priority, the contestants need to adapt, and this is particularly the case in Taekwon-Do where kicks feature so strongly because of their longer range and higher scoring capability. Given the fighters' understandable enthusiasm for kicking, it is hardly surprising that they tend to favour kicks over punches and come to expect their opponents to do the same. The result of this, in less experienced fighters, is often that they will trade turning kicks initially until one fighter steps forward and starts throwing punches to the head, which normally then leads to either the defender backing off into kicking range or both fighters abandoning any effective defence and engaging in an unfocused flurry of punches (few of which are normally scored). This lack of defence at short range is one of the commonest failings in Taekwon-Do and other 'traditional' kick-based martial arts, and the importance of adopting the short-range guard described in Chapter 4 cannot be emphasized strongly enough. With a strong guard and good body movement you can break out of this pattern by standing your ground and employing three basic defensive techniques.

Blocking

When blocking punches at short range it is most important to be as economical with your movement as possible (*see* first sequence opposite).

Incorrect Blocking at Short Range

Although this 'big' block stops the hook punch, the blocking arm is too high to …

… deflect the cross and the middle section is still unprotected against …

… a switch turning kick.

You must keep your movements short and tight to perform the block and then return to the guard in the shortest possible time (*see* sequence below).

As always, the best way to develop this economy of movement is to practise it in set drills where you know what is coming, such as the high-section hook and body shot combination used above that you can develop to make more challenging by adding a further punch to the combination (*see* sequence on page 72.)

The more you practise these and the other short-range defence drills that follow, the more comfortable you will become when faced with short-range attacks and the less you will (over)-react to each. The transition that you are seeking here is from no longer worrying too much about the first technique (and thereby being less

Correct Minimal Movement Blocking a Punch

A smaller blocking movement for the hook, and keeping the rear arm tighter to the body allows the defender to …

… block the follow-up cross more successfully and …

… the middle-section turning kick.

Sample Punch-Blocking Drill

The defender blocks the hook with the lead arm, ...

... blocks the cross with the rear arm and ...

... bobs to avoid the second hook.

effective in defending against follow-up punches and strikes), to your having the confidence to stand your ground and weather the storm while keeping sufficiently calm and alert to counter quickly and strongly. Blocking drills help you to develop this confidence because you will realize that you can, in fact, take quite powerful shots to your head and body on your arms without injury, but you will need to use it in combination with the other basic, short-range defensive techniques.

Parrying

In free sparring the term 'blocking' tends to refer mainly to defensive techniques that protect the defender and deflect attacks rather than to

actually preventing the technique from being completed by striking the attacking limb 'full-on', as do many of the blocks in more traditional Asian martial arts. At short range this type of blocking is called 'parrying' and differs from its traditional 'power' blocking counterpart by employing the same economy of movement described above. While absorbing attacks can be effective against hook punches and strikes to the head and the body, and to a degree against straight punches to the body, parrying is more effective against straight punches to the head such as the jab (*see* sequence opposite).

Correctly executed, parrying a high-section attack will disrupt your opponent sufficiently to

Lead-Hand Parrying

As the attacker starts to jab, the defender tucks his chin in further and positions the lead arm ...

... to parry the punch with minimal movement, allowing the lead hand to ...

... revert to the short-range guard position as quickly as possible.

create a momentary opening that you can best exploit with your fastest punch – your lead-hand jab; while your rear hand can be used for parrying, it should be held in reserve to handle your opponent's follow-up cross, which can then be worked into this useful drill (*see* first sequence on page 74).

Effective parrying is not easy and requires good timing and accuracy, and, even if you do not use it a great deal when sparring, these skills can be greatly developed through parrying and counter-attacking drills; again, your confidence will increase as you realize that you can actually intercept some fast, direct punches and respond instantly.

Evasion

Since Western boxing is primarily concerned with short-distance fighting, it recognizes a number of different types of short-range evasive movement, such as slipping, bobbing and weaving, and the time spent studying these individual techniques is well spent.

However, for the present it is sufficient to examine evasive body movement in general, where your goal is to avoid the attack directly if you can or at least to move in a way to minimize the effect of the punch without retreating (*see* second sequence on page 74).

Maintaining your guard, keeping your body moving and concentrating on your opponent

Drill for Parrying and Counter-Attacking

Immediately after parrying the attacker's jab, the defender …

… counters with a jab using the same hand and then …

… follows up with a cross using the rear hand.

Common Short-Range Evasion Techniques

Slipping a jab by moving to the side.

Bobbing underneath a hook.

Avoiding a jab by moving the body backwards.

Drill for Maintaining an Effective Guard

The defender stands with his rear foot against a wall so that he cannot move back.

The attacker then unleashes a series of jabs …

… and hooks …

… with the defender keeping his arms tightly together to absorb punches as well as …

… rolling the body to avoid them …

… and to add variety – throw in the odd front snap kick as well!

are the keys to success here, and the best single exercise to both improve all of these areas and to develop your confidence is to strip away every other defensive option than your body position and short-range guard under sustained attack (*see* sequence above).

For some, this may seem far from their idea of themselves sparring – 'acting as a punch bag'

and being unable to retaliate – but it is only by focusing completely on the basics of your guard and body movement that you will be able to stand your ground and move beyond your instinctive fight or flight reactions, and this is therefore the single most important exercise for your short-range defence. Start slowly with relatively light punches and gradually build up speed and intensity, drawing on all the defensive techniques including parrying and counter-attacking: the more you practise this drill the 'tighter' your defence will become, the fewer shots will connect with any power and the more your confidence in your short-range defence will improve. Of equal importance to the increased effectiveness of your defence to neutralize your opponent's attacks is the development of your mental attitude: apprehension about being hit gives way to irritation when a shot comes through as you realize that you can absorb the majority of the punches and that, when one does connect, it does no permanent damage. If your mind is straight away focusing on closing that 'gap' rather than dwelling on having been hit, then you are respectful of your opponent for his success but you no longer fear him and this is the best mental state from which to counter-attack effectively.

Attacking Defence

In all of the above, a strong emphasis has been placed on the importance of dealing with your opponent's attack through standing your ground or evasion and being in a good position to counter-attack. The periods during and immediately after an attack are often when your best scoring opportunities arise since your opponent has come to you and has had to compromise his guard when launching the attack, frequently abandoning it altogether, as described in Chapter 4. A key (and often neglected) part of your defence is to

Rear-Arm Position in Lead-Leg Kicks

By keeping the rear hand high …

… throughout a lead-leg kick you are …

… best placed to block a counter to your open side.

76

avoid making this same mistake and to compromise your defence as little as possible when you are attacking. Experience plays a large part here as you come to recognize the frequency of successful counter-attacks against particular techniques or combinations, but you can accelerate this process by extending your defensive attitude into your attacking strategy. Put yourself in your opponent's position and imagine that you are standing your ground in the face of your favourite attacks and looking to counter quickly and strongly: where are the weak spots? What would be the most effective counter-attack? Watch other people sparring: do you avoid creating the same openings when attacking? The chances are that you do not, or at least that you do not do so all the time.

While this on-going analysis of your own sparring style is personal to you, there are some basic points that you should always bear in mind, particularly early in your sparring development: *protect your chin!*

Your head in general, and your chin in particular, is your most vital target area and you must always preserve the function of the rear arm in both the standard and the short-range sparring guards when kicking and when punching.

Chin Protection when Kicking

All sparring kicks, including jumping kicks, require the supporting leg to be behind the attacking leg at the point of impact, either supporting the body on the ground or trailing the kicking leg in the air. Your open side is therefore always the side of your supporting or non-kicking leg and this is the side on which you should always seek to protect your chin with your rear arm as the kick is executed. In the case of a lead-leg kick, this requires that you do not drop your rear arm (*see* sequence opposite).

When you kick with the rear leg, your guard must change in the same way as when you step forwards or backwards (*see* sequence below). Remember, this applies for all kicks (*see* first sequence on page 78).

Rear-Arm Position in Rear-Leg Kicks

When kicking with the rear leg …

… change your guard round as soon as the kicking leg is committed …

… keeping the (now) rear hand held high, protecting the chin as the kick is executed and …

… in place to form the full guard after the kick is complete.

Rear-Arm Position in Various Kicks

Side kick.

Downward kick.

Front snap kick.

Chin Protection when Punching

The major difference when performing hand techniques as opposed to kicks is that you can perform attacks with either hand from the same stance, so, in order to best protect your chin, whichever arm is not attacking must come back to a guard position (*see* sequence below).

Alternate Guarding Arm when Punching

Rear arm is already in place for the jab but …

… the lead hand must be retracted immediately when starting the cross and …

… held in position as the punch is completed.

The protecting hand must be held in place throughout a jumping punch.

78

Part II
Core Techniques

Building on a sound defence and good body movement, effective Taekwon-Do sparring requires you to be able to use a range of techniques and strategies to handle different opponents with varying fighting styles. Given that there are literally thousands of techniques in Taekwon-Do, you need to select a smaller group of core techniques that cover the principal types of attack and that you can develop and change over time. This section presents just such a group of techniques that have been particularly successful for Master Hogan and his fighters. You may already use some of the techniques listed here or you may prefer others that are not – the purpose of this section is to provide a basic analysis of techniques that you can then use to help to refine your own core techniques. But remember: don't become too predictable … there is always room to try something new in sparring.

7 Hand Techniques

Although ITF Taekwon-Do is justifiably famous for its wide range of kicking techniques and a scoring system that encourages kicking over punching, over recent years hand techniques have overtaken kicks as the principal method of scoring in competition sparring. The fundamental reason for this lies in the considerable rise in the standard of sparring, due not only to more frequent and better attended competitions but also to the increased exposure of fighters to other martial arts through cross-training and open-style competitions. As standards have improved, opponents have become harder to hit and the speed of the hands over the legs makes it generally easier to score with punches at a closer range than with kicks at a longer range. But the speed advantage of hand techniques is not just confined to short

range – jumping punches and strikes have become increasingly popular since they not only close the distance between the fighters extremely quickly but they also score an additional point if they are delivered as high-section attacks.

When fighters are operating at close range their use of short-range punches and strikes is, by necessity, more instinctive since they must react quickly to a higher volume of attacks thrown in a shorter space of time than when at kicking distance; as discussed in the previous chapter, you need to get behind your guard and try to exploit/create openings for counter-attacks. But since your general objective is to score points with minimal danger to yourself, you should not actively seek to turn sparring bouts into short-range boxing matches (unless, of course, your

Footwork for Jumping Hand Techniques

Bend the knees slightly to …

… take off from the lead leg and …

… land on the same leg after completing the punch in the air.

Finally, shuffle forward immediately after the rear leg lands.

opponent is particularly weak at short range). This chapter therefore focuses on a few individual attacking and counter-attacking hand techniques that can be incorporated into your core attacking arsenal rather than toe-to-toe boxing strategies. If you are a fighter who uses his hands a lot then you should use some of these techniques as alternatives to the standard combinations, such as a stepping punch followed by a cross; if you tend not to use your hands much then you should start now and use some of these techniques to vary your rhythm and make you less predictable.

Jumping Hand Techniques

Jumping punches and strikes are great techniques that not only offer a high probability of scoring but also intimidate your opponent because of their speed, the distance covered and the difficulty in blocking them. But these benefits are based on the jump being quick enough and high enough (*see* sequence opposite).

Getting the jump right is the key to success – this 'hopping' method, where you take off and land on the same foot, allows you to develop height and distance without telegraphing the technique and should form a regular part of your footwork warm-up/training. With the correct jump in place, the following jumping punches and strikes are relatively straightforward.

Jumping Punches

An increasingly popular competition technique, jumping punches (and, indeed, jumping strikes) are unique to Asian martial arts (they are banned in Western boxing), where they enjoy a high scoring success rate because of their speed and 'unorthodoxy', but care must be taken immediately following the technique (*see* sequence below).

A good jump will close a considerable distance at great speed and the higher you can jump the more you can punch downward, surprising your opponent and making it harder for him to block.

Use

As with all techniques, distance and timing dictate when best to use a jumping punch, and, since you can make only a limited directional adjustment when you are actually in the air, you need to be

Lead-Hand Jumping Punch

The punch should ideally be delivered at the apex of the jump, but …

… as the attacker lands on the front foot he is close to his opponent and it is usual to shuffle forward and …

… pivot to put some distance between the attacker and his opponent.

surer of your opponent's location at the time of impact than when you are executing a ground-based attack. Therefore the best time to throw a jumping punch is when your opponent is static either through inactivity or indecision.

The obvious time to catch your opponent being inactive is right at the start of the bout when most fighters generally try to use the first few seconds to sum up their opponent – a jumping punch will close the distance quickly otherwise, and even if it does not score, it will disquiet your opponent (*see* sequence below).

While this strategy can also be successful at the start of the round or after a referee's intervention, it will not have as much surprise value as at the start and should therefore be used sparingly during the fight. However, an alternative to your waiting for your opponent's inactivity is to try and make him hesitate when advancing, and the best method for this is pivoting backwards, as shown

in the previous chapter. Correctly timed, this is a great technique since your opponent (although stopped momentarily) is committed to going forward and you (assuming that you pivoted correctly) are already primed to push off into the technique (*see* first sequence opposite).

The same strategy will work for any situation where you have caused your opponent to hesitate at reasonably long range. However, if your opponent is increasing the distance between you by stepping back after you have jumped, then you can still score by throwing the cross after the jab to try and make up the extra distance before you land (*see* second sequence opposite).

Equally, if you find that your opponent is closing the distance by advancing after you have started to jump or is just simply closer, then you can shorten the range of the technique by swapping the lead-hand punch for the reverse punch (*see* sequence on page 84).

Extending the Length of Attack: Jumping Punch from the Ready Position

Opponents face each other at the starting distance – ...

... a slight dip of the knees is enough to power a jump to ...

... close the distance and score with a lead-hand jumping punch.

Pivoting Backwards with Jumping-Punch Counter-Attack

As the opponent
advances and …

… the defender pivots on
the front foot – as soon as
the rear foot touches the
ground, he jumps forward
on the front foot …

… with a high-section lead-
hand jumping punch.

Jumping Lead and Reverse Punch for Extra Distance

The opponent moves away as the
attacker start to jump and …

… avoids the attacker's lead-
hand jumping punch but …

… is still in range for the follow-up
jumping reverse punch.

Jumping Reverse Punch for a Shorter Range

As the opponent starts to …

… move in closer to punching range …

… a jumping reverse punch is a good counter at shorter range.

Practice

Other than practising the particular actions shown above, the best routine to develop your timing and range for throwing the jumping punch is to train with your partner in rounds of a minimum of a minute's length in which the attacker must chase the 'target' of the opponent's raised glove (*see* first sequence onpposite).

Jumping Hand Strikes

While jumping punches are generally used to the best effect when you are trying to close the distance between yourself and your opponent in a straight line, the surprise element of the jump and the downward trajectory of the technique can still be used to attack the side of your opponent's head at closer range by using a variety of hand strikes instead of direct punches. The commonest jumping-hand strike in use today is the jumping back-fist strike (*see* second sequence opposite).

The back-fist strike is a confusing enough technique to block on the ground with the attacking arm moving (initially) in the opposite direction from the strike, but when combined with a good jump it can be extremely difficult to block. At shorter range, an effective and underused technique is the jumping reverse knife-hand strike that has the advantages of being difficult to spot with its long, arcing motion and offering a longer range than a hooking punch (*see* first sequence on page 86).

Drill to Improve the Timing and Distance of a Jumping Punch

With both fighters in motion …

… the defender stops and raises his hand as a target for …

… the attacker to execute a jumping punch immediately, then repeat, etc.

Jumping Back-Fist Strike

A good set-up for the technique is to …

… quickly side-step before …

… jumping in with a lead-hand back-fist strike to the temple.

85

Jumping Reverse Knife-Hand Strike

This technique needs no set-up and can be launched with the attacker directly facing the defender …

… to target the temple.

Use

Both these jumping strikes (and others) are particularly effective as fast counter-attacks at medium range, and your best opportunity, as with the jumping punch, is when your opponent is static, such as just after he has scored or (we hope more often) just after you have checked his advance through blocking or avoiding his attack. Put yourself in your opponent's position to best understand the advantages of this counter: at the end of an advance you have just delivered your favourite technique and you are now at closer range behind a strong guard, bracing yourself for (most likely) a punch-based counter-attack

Jumping Back-Fist Counter-Attack

Immediately after a successful inward block of a long-range kick, the defender is …

… side-facing the attacker and ideally placed to jump high and …

… counter-attack with a jumping back-fist strike to the opponent's closed side temple.

and, instead, an attack is coming downwards on to your temple! Speed is of the essence here – at that moment of relative inactivity after an attack you must jump as high and as quickly as you can and get your strike in before your opponent has realized what is happening (*see* second sequence opposite).

When you find yourself positioned more directly in front of your opponent, the reverse knife-hand strike with the rear hand is much harder to spot (*see* sequence below).

Again, use this technique sparingly – if your opponent can predict that you will retaliate with a jumping reverse knife-hand strike he will find a way to take advantage of it. But it is an eye-catching, high-scoring and unusual technique … perhaps best left to the closing stages of the fight.

Practice

For the present, your interest in jumping hand strikes is as quick reaction, closer-range counter-attacks and you need to set up drills with your partner where he steps in with an attack, you block or evade and counter instantly with whichever jumping hand strike seems to fit best. Change the attack, the counter, your stance and your opponent's stance until you find which block

and counter combinations work for you – these are the ones that you then need to practise.

Reverse Punch

Although much loved as a fast counter-punch in karate, the reverse or cross punch is less popular in Taekwon-Do sparring. This is mainly due to the scoring system where all hand techniques (other than high-section jumping techniques) score only a single point, so the temptation is to neglect the body and concentrate on high-section punches and strikes that are more likely to be seen and therefore scored by the corner judges. While your objective is to score points as efficiently as possible within the rules, it is nonetheless important not to be overwhelmed by the rules to the extent that you miss the point of what you are doing. Taekwon-Do is a martial art where your first priority is self-defence and you need to be able to handle yourself outside the tournament ring, where it may well not be possible to throw multiple jumping reverse turning kicks to your opponent's head! If you have ever been on the receiving end of a powerful reverse punch to your solar plexus, you will know why it is so popular in single-point sparring: correctly delivered, it is a devastating technique

Jumping Reverse Knife-Hand Counter-Attack

Countering the long-range kick with a more orthodox block …

… leaves the defender directly facing the attacker and therefore better placed to counter with …

… a jumping reverse knife-hand strike.

that is difficult to spot and that can easily drop you if you are unprepared. So, to round off this chapter on hand techniques, we are going to make a plea for the reverse punch – it may not attract many points but it can be extremely effective … and your opponent will almost certainly not be expecting it.

Blitzing

Most Taekwon-Do fighters would never open a bout with a stepping reverse punch, but there is a way of combining the technique with some intelligent footwork that, correctly performed, is almost guaranteed to score: the 'blitz'.

The blitz works on two fundamental principles: speed and the difficulty of your opponent in concentrating on more than one thing at a time – in this case you are getting him to focus on your footwork (*see* sequence below).

The key is in the pulling back of your front foot: it must be a sufficiently bold movement to catch your opponent's eye for the split second you need in which to step forward immediately with your rear leg – executed correctly, the reverse punch will seem to come from nowhere (*see* sequence opposite).

Use

A good time to try this technique is right at the start of the bout, but it can be executed at any time when your opponent is sizing you up at just outside kicking range. Why? While it is possible to over-analyse techniques, the psychology employed here serves as a useful prelude to the final section of the book – you are working against your opponent's expectations. At this range, he is either contemplating his own next advance or one from you: in the case of the latter he expects you either to start to step forward or begin to raise a leg for a kick, but, instead, he sees your front foot go back slightly. Are you retreating? If so, why before an attack has been launched? What should he do next? The point is that your opponent cannot avoid noticing your foot movement in the absence of anything else happening – the movement is ambiguous and it is difficult to react to instantly … and that is your opportunity to strike. Using the reverse punch further adds to the confusion since by far the commoner technique would be a stepping punch; other techniques such as a reverse back fist might also work but none can match the speed and power of the reverse punch.

Footwork for the Blitz

From the sparring stance …

… draw the lead foot back sharply about 6in …

… step forward with your rear leg and then ….

… step forward again, throwing the reverse punch as you do so.

Reverse Punch Blitz

The initial move of the foot draws your opponent's attention, while …

… the first step 'contradicts' the backward movement, confusing the defender and …

… setting him up for the next step and reverse punch.

Practice

Although simple to describe, this is a difficult technique to master. It relies on good movement, accurate timing and, above all, commitment. Since the blitz depends on the credibility of the initial lead-foot movement – it needs to be just right: significant enough to provoke a reaction in your opponent but not so exaggerated as to impede your forward motion; you need to be observed by an experienced fighter since your partner's reaction is inevitably affected by the fact that he knows what's coming. Once you get the initial movement right then work on your speed, that is, reaching the target as soon as possible – you must score with your punch before your opponent realizes that the immediate danger is not from your feet but from your rapidly advancing fist. But really this is one of those techniques that can only be perfected by use in actual sparring conditions; try and commit to it at least once during a fight and, once you get it right, try not to use it all the time.

Reverse Punch Counter-Attacking

As previously stated, it is as a fast counter-punch that the reverse punch is used so extensively in karate sparring, and with good reason. Coming from the rear, it is harder to spot and can accelerate more than the jab, thereby delivering more power. The natural target for the reverse punch is your opponent's middle section as it becomes exposed during and just after an attack, and, because you want to counter as fast as possible, you need to modify the technically 'correct' punch to your purposes (*see* first sequence on page 90).

Use

Although not a high-scoring technique (only a single point) and not a highly 'visible' one (that is, the corner judges may well not see it since it is so close quarters), this is a great technique with which to upset your opponent. If you can make this truly 'reactive', so that whenever your opponent is in close after an attack he immediately receives a strong counter-punch to his solar plexus, it will force him to change his approach, if not necessarily accumulate many points against him. In short, this is best viewed as an intimidating technique to modify your opponent's behaviour just at the point that his confidence should be at its height (*see* second sequence on page 90).

Reverse Punch Counter-Attack

As the opponent closes in …

… the defender extends his lead arm both to confuse attacker and generate more power when …

… dropping and twisting the body to deliver the reverse punch – note the lead hand covering the chin and the raising of the rear heel and slight turning out of the lead foot to further increase the power of the punch.

Practice

Maintaining a proper guard and good timing are essential here and one of the best ways to improve both is to modify the Taekwon-Do one-step sparring exercise, where the attacker can throw any technique he wants – the defender's objective is to get in a strong reverse punch counter-attack as fast as possible, preferably blocking or avoiding the attack at the same time.

Opportunities for Reverse Punch Counter-Attack

Stepping to the side to avoid a turning kick presents a good reverse punch opportunity.

Deflecting a side kick and turning the attacker …

… creates an opportunity for a fast high section counter that is difficult to see coming.

8   Lead-Leg Kicks

Most ITF Taekwon-Do kicks can be performed with either the lead or the rear leg and they are normally taught as such (that is, as twin aspects of the same kick); however, just as with a punch, the use of the lead or rear limb changes the character of the attack as much as the jab differs from the cross. Alongside the basic differences between lead- and rear-leg kicks, such as speed and power, distance and strategy considerations can often require modification of the 'standard' technique to the extent that the lead-leg version of, for instance, a side kick differs sufficiently from that of a rear-leg side kick that they can reasonably be seen (and taught) as separate and distinct techniques – and this is the approach taken here.

Lead-leg kicks are a critical element in a fighter's arsenal since they allow him to attack at a middle distance (just outside punching range and too close for rear-leg kicks) and are therefore equally useful when pressing an attack or counter-attacking. Whatever the kick, the single most important success factor is speed – reactive speed to create/spot the opportunity and execution speed to score. Of course, this is true of all sparring techniques, but when operating at just outside punching range your lead-leg kicks need to be particularly fast in order to score before your opponent steps in with his inherently faster hand techniques or beats you to it with his own lead-leg kick. In order to develop superior speed, you need to work on a number of core lead-leg kick techniques and make them become more instinctive, not only by extensive practice but also by appropriate modification. This chapter covers the core lead-leg kicks that have scored most frequently in competitive Taekwon-Do sparring over recent years and explains how

they can best be modified to improve speed and scoring likelihood; again, the list is not exhaustive or exclusive, but some of these techniques should be at the heart of your sparring arsenal.

Side Kick

The standard lead-leg side kick requires a significant degree of technical proficiency and flexibility to execute well (*see* first sequence on page 92).

While it can be (like its rear-leg counterpart) a powerful attack, it is relatively slow and requires good hip flexibility. A proficient side-kicker can use it to his advantage with the pump side-kick technique, where the lead leg is continuously chambered and multiple kicks fired out – this can be an both an effective defensive and attacking strategy (*see* second sequence on page 92).

However, effective pump side-kickers are the exception (and when you meet them you must cut the distance down by advancing at 45 degrees inside their kick on their open side) and the standard side kick does not generally suit most fighters in sparring. An alternative and easier lead-leg, straight-line kick is the front snap or pushing kick, but this has the twin drawbacks of limited range and a poor defensive position and is seldom seen in competition sparring. However, with minor adjustment, the side kick can become significantly faster and easier to execute while retaining its greater range and defensive posture, thereby providing a vital lead-leg, straight-line attack for most fighters.

The principal adjustment that needs to be made is to increase the speed of the kick by making the trajectory of the attacking tool (the heel and the

The Standard Lead-Leg Side Kick

| The kicking leg must be chambered close to the body at kicking height. | Then the hips must be turned over slightly so that … | … the kicking foot can travel in a straight line until … | … it can lock out on the target. |

Pump Side Kicking

The attacker balances on his rear leg while executing …

… one or more side kicks, then …

… sliding forward and executing more side kicks.

outer edge of the foot) more direct (*see* sequence below).

Now the kick is not only quicker and requires less hip flexibility but it is also less signalled because the leg is not fully chambered and the kick is travelling upwards rather than straight out from the hip. The range at which the kick is delivered requires a further modification to the extent to which the kicking leg is locked out, creating two basic variants.

Closer-Range, Lead-Leg Side Kick

The fastest kick travels the least distance to its target and, in the case of the lead-leg side kick, this can be achieved by not fully extending the kick into the target when kicking at closer range (*see* first sequence on page 94).

With the side kick it is particularly important that you re-chamber the leg quickly and either deliver another kick or return to your sparring stance; a common weakness is that the stance is compromised after the delivery of the kick if the hip is not fully retracted to its default position.

Use

The speed and 'stopping' ability of this kick make it an ideal counter-attacking technique to check your opponent's advance, particularly when he is more full-facing and presenting you with the largest possible middle-section target, typically in mid-stride when he is stepping forward (*see* second sequence on page 94).

Although this kick can be used at any stage during your opponent's advance, since it requires accurate timing at quite close range, it is often most effective when you are 'waiting' for your opponent (that is, you are static and he is in motion), typically just at the start of his advance as he takes his first step. Another situation where the kick can be particularly useful is when you are retreating under pressure and find yourself with your rear foot on the edge of the ring without sufficient range to throw a rear-leg kick; correctly delivered, the kick can push your opponent back, providing an opportunity for you to escape.

Lead-Leg Side Kick Modified for Speed

The knee rises forward, not straight up to the body.

The hip turns as the lead leg rises, not once it reaches kicking height.

The foot reaches the target coming up from the ground rather than out from the hip.

Partially Extended Lead-Leg Side Kick

With the opponent at closer range …

… the kick does not lock out on impact.

Use the resistance of the opponent's body to push back, retract the kick quickly and resume sparring stance.

Timing of Lead-Leg Side Kick at Closer Range

As the opponent starts to advance …

… transfer weight to the back leg and …

… deliver the kick before the opponent has finished his step.

Drill to Improve Speed and Timing of Closer-Range, Lead-Leg Side Kick

Kicker stands his ground as …   … the opponent advances, forming a …   … middle-section target for a close-range side kick.

Practice

As always, speed and timing are key to the success of this kick and this is a simple drill to help you to develop both (*see* sequence above).

Longer-Range, Lead-Leg Side Kick

By fully extending the lead leg, the range of the kick is increased, making it more suitable for launching an attack as opposed to counter-attacking (*see* sequence below).

Fully Extended, Lead-Leg Side Kick

At the edge of kicking range …   … the lead-leg side kick can reach the target by …

… fully extending the kicking leg.

Using a sliding action with the rear leg to extend the range still further is particularly effective with the side kick (*see* sequence below).

Use

Although faster than the standard side kick, the locking out of the leg makes the kick somewhat slower than the closer-range version described earlier, and it is probably best to use it sparingly in any single bout. It is a good 'feeler' kick to test your opponent's middle-section guard at the start of the fight, particularly when using the slide shown above, allowing you to come out of attacking range and then return by shuffling backwards after the kick. Otherwise your best opportunities are likely to be the same when pressing an attack as they are when counter-attacking, that is, when your opponent is more full-facing, such as when he is retreating in mid-stride. But if your opponent is an experienced fighter with a good guard you are unlikely to score with this technique alone – combining it with a feint to the high section is often more successful (*see* Part III).

Practice

Since the kick itself is merely a full extension of the previous kick, your practice should focus on gaining the maximum distance by increasing the range in the previous drill.

Turning Kick

As with the lead-leg side kick, the standard lead-leg turning kick (although extremely popular) is actually quite a difficult kick to perform correctly (*see* first sequence opposite).

Sliding to Further Extend the Lead-Leg Side Kick

At longer range, the lead-leg side kick …

… can be further extended by starting to slide on the rear leg as the attacker begins the kick and …

… continues sliding until the point of impact.

The Standard Lead-Leg Turning Kick

In the standard lead-leg turning kick, the leg is chambered at 90 degrees to the body and …

… then comes round in an arc parallel to the floor before …

… extending the ball of the foot into the target at an angle of 45 degrees.

Again, some adjustments are required to make the kick faster, less telegraphed and more practical for use in sparring. The first change that is required is to adapt the kick for a more direct-facing target – although the kick can be effective should you find yourself at 45 degrees to your opponent, in practice, it is more frequently going to be used when your opponent is in front of you. This, in turn, changes the extent to which it is necessary to turn your hips into the kick and the part of the foot that you kick with (the ball of the foot being less useful when you are wearing foot protectors in any case). Finally, for speed and surprise, the kick must travel directly forwards, with no chambering of the leg (*see* sequence below).

Lead-Leg Turning Kick Modified for Speed and Angle of Attack

The kick starts from the ground with the kicking leg coming straight up and …

… the hips turning only in the latter stages as the kick …

… extends (usually) the instep into the target straight ahead.

Targets for Middle-Section, Lead-Leg Turning Kick

With more of a turn of the hips and using the ball of the foot, the solar plexus is the traditional middle-section target, but …

… with slightly less rotation of the hips and kicking with the instep, the floating ribs become the target.

In effect (and similar to the lead-leg side kick), the kick is now a hybrid of a front kick and a turning kick which makes it harder to read and, with practice, extremely fast for use as both a middle- and a high-section attack.

Middle-Section, Lead-Leg Turning Kick

This is an excellent kick to have in your arsenal since it not only attacks the traditional middle-section target of the solar plexus but it also opens up a new and highly vulnerable target area – the floating ribs (*see* sequence above).

Use

The best type of opponent for this kick is one who holds his guard quite high, presenting you with an easy target for an unexpected shot to his floating ribs, particularly when he is more forward- than side-facing; equally, an opponent who raises his front arm to block a high-section attack presents a perfect opportunity (*see* first sequence opposite).

Once mastered, this is a kick that you will find yourself using instinctively whenever the opportunity presents itself (or can be created) and it can be particularly effective against opponents who are more rooted in 'traditional' sparring techniques. Speed, of course, is essential but this is

a kick where you need to get some power behind it since you cannot rely on your opponent's body mass moving into the kick and he needs to know that he has been hit or he is just going to walk through it the next time you throw it.

Practice

Picking up on the last point, the drill shown opposite will help you to develop power, accuracy and stamina (*see* second sequence opposite).

High-Section, Lead-Leg Turning Kick

If you have the flexibility, then to be able to kick to the side of the head at relatively close quarters is a useful skill and this faster lead-leg turning kick is the best way to score those two points, but note that the hips must turn further in order to plant the kick into the side of your opponent's head rather than just 'glance' the target (*see* sequence on page 100).

Use

Here your ideal opponent is one who holds his guard low but, as with the middle-section lead-leg turning kick, if you can execute the kick quickly and accurately then there will be no shortage of opportunities. However, beware of its overuse

Opportunities for Middle-Section, Lead-Leg Turning Kick

Against an opponent with a high, classic karate guard, it is easy to target the floating ribs under the guard.

If an opponent blocks too high then he leaves himself exposed under his blocking arm to …

… a kick to the floating ribs.

Drill for Developing the Middle-Section, Lead-Leg Turning Kick

The attacker kicks the defender's target on the lead hip of the rear hand on top of the lead hand, then…

… the attacker switches stance, the defender switches target and …

… the attacker kicks a new target with the other leg.

High-Section, Lead-Leg Turning Kick

As the leg rises above the middle section ...

... the hips turn enough ...

... to allow the extended foot to
strike the target more directly.

because this kick can leave you more exposed
and an experienced opponent will be quick to
counter strongly if he can read the kick coming.
Try varying the side that you kick to during a bout
– kick to the open side at closer range and to the
closed side when further back.

Practice

To train for kicking to both sides you can vary the
previous drill (*see* first sequence opposite).

Hooking Kick

The lead-leg hooking kick is an excellent, shorter-
range technique that is both hard to spot and hard
to block as it starts low and changes character,
with its snapping motion at end of the attack (*see*
second sequence opposite).

Since this kick is executed at closer range than
the majority of others, it is most important that
you resume your sparring stance and back off
quickly if you are not going to pursue the attack
with another, short-range technique. The kick can
be used against both high- and middle-section
targets with no modification other than the height
but the target generally dictates the nature of the
attack.

High-Section, Lead-Leg Hooking Kick

This is a good, closer-range attacking technique
that has all the advantages already stated, plus an
additional element of surprise in that most people
revert to hand techniques when at (or close to)
punching range, but you do need to have quite
a high degree of flexibility in the hips (*see* first
sequence on page 102).

Drill for Developing High-Section, Lead-Leg Turning Kick

With both fighters in the same stance, the attacker kicks to the defender's head on his open side …

… then both fighters switch stance and …

… the attacker kicks with the other leg to the defender's new open side.

The Lead-Leg Hooking Kick

The lead leg comes up and slightly …

… across the body before …

… snapping the heel (or ball of foot) sharply into the target.

101

High-Section, Lead-Leg Hooking Kick

As the attacker's leg comes up, it is …

… difficult to predict the type of kick …

… until the final hooking motion of the foot.

Use

This is a deceptive attacking technique that works best when you are at closer range and your opponent is expecting a hand attack. You can enhance this expectation by throwing or feinting a hand technique to the other side of your opponent's head (*see* sequence below).

Practice

To score with this technique you need to get in close quickly, deliver the kick accurately and back off immediately – this drill works on these three aspects (*see* first sequence opposite).

Middle-Section, Lead-Leg Hooking Kick

When the kick is delivered to the middle section you have a slightly longer range that requires less flexibility (*see* second sequence opposite).

Use

While this can occasionally be used as an attack, it is best used as a rapid counter-attack when your opponent is advancing towards you (*see* third sequence opposite).

Practice

To get the feel for the range and timing of this counter-attack you need to work on the full range of distances to your attacker. Try to develop free-form drills where your opponent steps in from:

- a longer range where you need to shuffle in to meet him
- a short range where you remain in the same spot
- an even shorter range where you need to shuffle back to get the range.

Creating an Opportunity for High-Section, Lead-Leg Hooking Kick

The attacker's jab draws the defender's guard …

… and the kick starts just as the punch is ending to …

… attack the defender's head on his closed side.

Drill for High-Section, Lead-Leg Hooking Kick

The attacker comes into closer range, already starting a …

… high-section, lead-leg hooking kick and then …

… shuffling back out of range as quickly as possible.

Middle-Section, Lead-Leg Hooking Kick

Again, the kick is hard to read in the early stages …

… and it is particularly useful in exploiting …

… 'sideways' gaps in the defender's guard.

Opportunity for Middle-Section, Lead-Leg Hooking Kick

A good opportunity is when your opponent strides forwards and …

… does not change his guard quickly and tightly enough.

103

9 Rear-Leg Kicks

Powerful and capable of scoring at long range, rear-leg kicks are the heavy artillery of all kick-based martial arts and, correctly executed, they can allow you to inflict maximum damage at minimum risk to yourself. They therefore occupy a central role in effective Taekwon-Do sparring since they give you more options: to score and back off, to pursue your opponent as he tries to retreat out of range, to provide an opening for closer-range techniques and to counter-attack as early as possible. There is, of course, a downside and that is the sacrifice of speed for this increased power and range – the longer your rear leg has to travel to the target, the slower the kick will be and the greater the chance of your opponent avoiding or counter-attacking. While there will always be exceptions, for most of the time it is the relatively faster and less telegraphed kicks that score the most and this chapter concentrates on a few core kicks that have these qualities.

Turning Kick

This kick is at the heart of most club-level sparring for all the reasons mentioned in previous chapters and, when performed with the rear leg, it can be a powerful and intimidating kick. As with the lead-leg turning kick, the standard kick needs to be modified in the same way for speed by omitting the chambering of the leg and for a frontal target by generally less (although not in all cases, as stated below) twisting of the hips (*see* below).

Rear-Leg Turning Kick Modified for Speed and Angle of Attack

The rear leg comes up in a ...

... straight line with minimal turning of the hips ...

... until the final extension of the ball of the foot or instep into the target.

While there are many similarities with the lead-leg version of the kick, there are some important variations in use for high- and middle-section attacks.

Middle-Section, Rear-Leg Turning Kick

Kicking to the floating ribs and to the solar plexus with the rear leg are identical to the use of the front leg, except that it is considerably more powerful, but there is also a strong case for reintroducing more hip twist in order to deliver a particularly powerful kick (*see* sequence below).

This kick allows you to deliver more power than you might ordinarily do since the referee will see none of the excessive penetration of, for instance, a strong, fully extended side kick or of the potential knock-out of a badly controlled head shot. Why should this be important? Although Taekwon-Do sparring is a semi-contact sport and must always be performed with an appropriate degree of self-control, that does not mean that it is merely a game of 'tag,' where all strikes are delivered at the same level of control. In practice, you need to operate within a range, sometimes exercising greater control when delivering potentially damaging actions, such as high-section, reverse turning, which can easily break an opponent's jaw if delivered close to full power, and sometimes not quite so much control when the risk of injury is smaller. This technique falls into the latter category and lets your opponent know that you can generate more power if you want to.

Use

There are two main uses for this more powerful middle-section attack, one strategic and the other tactical. When you are facing a new opponent and you are trying to gauge his ability and style in the early stages of a bout, this is an excellent kick to use to test his resilience, even if you are not necessarily going to score because he maintains a strong guard. You can learn a lot from his reaction: does he shrug it off? Is he intimidated? Does he respond in kind? Does he lose his temper? This analysis of your opponent is discussed in detail in the final section of the book.

The other principal use of this kick is as a strong counter-attack, particularly against a more aggressive and forceful opponent. To be used sparingly, perhaps only a couple of time in a bout, this is particularly effective in the situation described in Chapter 6, when pivoting backwards to avoid your

Middle-Section, Rear-Leg Turning Kick

In addition to the added momentum due to the greater distance travelled by the rear leg ...

... further power can be generated by turning the hips more into the target ...

... as the kick is completed.

opponent's advance/attack and you find yourself at longer range, mirroring your opponent's stance. What you are looking for is a momentary hesitation by your opponent in which to counter-attack strongly with this kick – this can happen solely as a result of your pivoting quickly and being seen to be ready or by feinting with a small body movement (again, covered in the final section); but however it is achieved, this split second when your opponent is static gives you the time you need to execute this more powerful, but slightly slower, middle-section rear-leg turning kick to maximum effect.

Practice

To develop the kick with more hip turning, the drill for the middle-section, lead-leg turning kick from the previous chapter can be easily adapted to develop speed and accuracy (*see* sequence below).

However, to develop increased power, you need to hit the target at full power and the gloves need to be swapped for the heavy bag or kick pad (*see* first sequence opposite).

High-Section, Rear-Leg Turning Kick

Similar to the lead-leg version, this is a popular kick with those that have the necessary flexibility since it allows you to score two points at longer range with minimal risk, and, even if your opponent reads it correctly, he is forced to react as he cannot 'wear' the kick if it is on target. This kick tends to be thrown more often than it scores and experienced fighters will have a strategy for dealing with it; you must therefore retract the leg quickly to limit your exposure to counter-attack (*see* second sequence opposite).

Drill for Middle-Section, Rear-Leg Turning Kick

The attacker kicks a smaller target – a single hand – making sure that his foot makes contact at a 90-degree angle to the target ...

... and switches stance after the kick in order to kick ...

... the other target with the new rear leg.

Pad Drill for Middle-Section, Rear-Leg Turning Kick

The defender braces the kick pad firmly against his forearms and …

… the attacker lets the kick go with maximum hip turn, quickly …

… retracting the kicking leg back into the sparring stance.

High-Section, Rear-Leg Turning Kick

After completing the kick, make sure to retract the leg as fast as possible by …

… bending it quickly back from the knee (which also gives you the option of delivering a follow-up, consecutive kick) before …

… withdrawing the whole kicking leg back into sparring stance.

Punch to Set Up High-Section, Rear-Leg Turning Kick

The attacker steps in with a punch to ...

... force the defender to step back and change his guard, creating an opening for ...

... a high-section, rear-leg turning kick.

Use

The problem with this kick is that it is relatively easy to read since the leg travels the greatest distance of all the turning kicks and, once you have thrown it, your opponent will find it even easier to read the next time. However, if you are quick and have good flexibility, it can make a good surprise opening attack; otherwise a situation where it can be particularly effective is to set your opponent up with a hand technique that distracts him and makes him alter his guard (*see* sequence above).

Practice

You need to make your high-section turning kick as fast and as accurate as you can, and, if you are not 'naturally' flexible, then you need to practise the basic kick (*see* sequence opposite).

Back Kick

Over recent years the back kick has become increasingly popular on the Taekwon-Do international competition circuit due to its speed, power, deceptiveness and excellent defensive body position – it is one of the most effective, straight-line, middle-section kicks and it should be in every Taekwon-Do fighter's repertoire.

When performed on the spot in a typical martial arts class, the back kick can, compared with other, 'easier' kicks, such as the turning kick, seem slow and cumbersome, but when used in sparring it becomes a surprisingly versatile kick that can be used at both close and long range and can be equally effective for both attack and counter-attack when using the standard kick and a specialized version, the switch back kick, as described below.

Drill for High-Section, Rear-Leg Turning Kick

The attacker kicks high section with the rear leg, retracts the leg and …

… both fighters switch stance then …

… the attacker kicks on the other side with the other leg.

Standard Back Kick

No modification is required to the standard back kick to make it an effective sparring technique, where the 'overhead' of turning the body 180 degrees is more than compensated for by the speed and directness of the kick itself (*see* first sequence on page 110).

However, before looking at the kick in more detail, it is worth noting that what many martial artists think is a back kick is, in fact, a side back kick, and, while it has its place in the multitude of Taekwon-Do kicks, it is less powerful and much easier to block and avoid (*see* second sequence on page 110).

The difference between the two is crucial and you must ensure that, when executing the back kick, your kicking leg extends in a straight line for maximum speed and power. In the authors'

experience, many Taekwon-Do students find it difficult to recognize that they are performing a side back kick instead of a back kick, and the habit persists, so get a colleague to video your back kick – the camera does not lie and you may well find that you need to correct your technique.

Use

If you can execute a fast and accurate back kick then it can make a very effective instant counter-attack (*see* first sequence on page 111).

But the kick becomes much easier to deliver and harder to read when you are in motion and the long range of the kick can be used to its best advantage, such as when your opponent is retreating out of range (*see* second sequence on page 111).

Standard Back Kick

Starting from a sparring stance, pivot towards your open side on the balls of both feet ...

... looking over the rear shoulder once the back is facing the target and the kicking leg starts to move back, while ...

... bending the knee to chamber the kick and ...

... finally thrust the leg straight out, making contact with the heel on the target.

Side Back Kick

From the same starting position, the most common fault is to ...

... lift the knee away from the body as the kicking leg rises, resulting in ...

... the kick taking a longer, more tangential route to the same target.

Instant Counter-Attack with Back Kick

As the attacker moves in, the defender pivots …

… towards his open side …

… to catch the attacker with a fast back kick to the middle section (note the strong defensive position of the kicker).

Forward Stepping Attack with Back Kick

As the defender starts to retreat under attack …

… the attacker steps forward and pivots…

… catching the retreating defender with the long range of the back kick.

111

Backward Stepping Counter-Attack with Back Kick

As the defender steps back from an attack …

… he starts to pivot as his rear foot lands …

… and completes the kick just as the attacker's front foot lands after his attack.

Basic Back Kick Drill

With both fighters in motion …

… one drops his arms as he stops to …

… form a target for the other to back kick immediately.

Equally effective is the reverse situation where you are retreating and you can use the kick as a long-range counter-attack (*see* first sequence opposite).

Practice

The back kick does not come naturally to most people and needs correspondingly more practice of the fundamental technique and its timing – this simple drill should form the basis of your back-kick training (*see* second sequence opposite).

You can then adapt this basic drill to incorporate taking one or even two steps forward or backward.

Switch Back Kick

This simple variation on the standard back kick not only allows the kick to be used at shorter range but also makes it significantly quicker and therefore a highly effective counter-attack (*see* below).

Note that this is not a jump but merely a fast switch of stance and orientation – this is an important point because the switch is the fastest possible way to deliver the back kick, whereas a jump, while it might be used to cover a greater distance (*see* the next chapter on jumping kicks), is slower.

Use

The primary use of the switch back kick is to shorten the range at which the back kick can be used by moving the body backwards while throwing the kick (*see* first sequence on page 114).

Practice

Again, this is a difficult (but extremely worth-while) technique to master and you must get the fundamentals right with a basic drill (*see* second sequence on page 114).

Once you have got the basics of the technique, this is a kick that works particularly well after one or more steps, as you 'draw' your opponent in closer with each step – try kicking after two steps and then three steps from your partner.

Switch Back Kick

From a sparring stance ...	... pivot to the open side on ball of the rear foot and, at the same time, draw the front foot towards the rear foot.	As the front foot approaches the rear foot and the pivot is complete, start to kick with the rear leg (note: this is while the front foot is still in motion) and ...	... complete the kick by extending the rear leg as the front foot stops moving.

Opportunity for Switch Back Kick

The attacker steps forward and …

… the defender starts to pivot …

… catching the attacker with a switch back kick before the attacker's technique is complete.

Drill for Switch Back Kick

Timing is key and you must start to …

… pivot as soon as the attacker moves in to …

… form a target for the defender to kick.

Hooking Kick

In addition to offering the same advantages as the lead-leg hooking kick but at longer range, the rear-leg hooking kick requires less hip flexibility and is therefore a more practicable option for the majority of fighters.

Although slower than its lead-leg version, the kick retains the same degree of deceptiveness, and, even if you can manage to kick only to the middle section, you should try to include this kick in your sparring repertoire. Also, the use of the rear leg gives the kick greater momentum, and a vigorous snap back of the lower leg can make this a powerful technique (*see* sequence below).

Rear-Leg Hooking Kick

The rear leg is raised in a forward direction …	… and as it comes forward of the body the hips turn so that …	… the leg as it extends is at an angle towards the kicker's open side …	… before the foot is snapped back sharply into the target.

Counter-Attack with High-Section, Rear-Leg Hooking Kick

An opponent stepping in sees the defender's rear-leg raise …

… and cannot read (and, indeed, is confused by) the kick …

… until the (too) fast later stage.

Use

The increased range allows for the same opportunities as the lead-leg hooking kick but taken at a greater distance. In addition, being able to throw the high-section kick from further away creates a particularly effective two-point counter-attack against an opponent stepping in with a low guard ((see second sequence on page 115).

Practice

You can adapt the drills for the lead-leg kick to handle the same situations and it is worth creating a simple drill based on the above to develop the high-section counter-attack.

Reverse Turning Kick

A technically difficult rear-leg technique, the reverse turning kick is a powerful (and not infrequently match-stopping) kick that, if used sparingly and with correct timing, can confuse and demoralize your opponent as he receives a strong blow from the edge of his peripheral vision (see sequence below).

The kick can be delivered to both middle- and high-section targets and the attacking tool can be varied to further extend its range (see first sequence oopposite).

Use

As with the rear-leg, high-section turning kick, this can make an effective surprise opening move at the start of a bout or, indeed, anywhere where your opponent is expecting something more 'direct', a typical opportunity being after a series of similar kicks, such as lead-leg or rear-leg turning kicks. Another good example of taking advantage of the surprise element of the kick is when it is used as a counter-attack after blocking a technique (see second sequence opposite).

Reverse Turning Kick

Pivot towards the open side on the ball of the front foot ...

... twisting the upper body and head round faster than the rear leg.

As the hips come round past 180 degrees, the kicking leg is held straight and allowed to rise as the hips continue to turn until ...

... the foot makes contact with the target straight ahead.

Options for Reverse Turning Kick

The heel can attack the middle section …

… or the high section, where …

… using the ball of the foot can extend the range of the kick.

Counter-Attack with Reverse Turning Kick

After blocking the attacker's kick …

… the defender pivoting and showing his back is confusing to the attacker who will not normally then be anticipating …

… a high-section, reverse turning kick.

Practice

Given the power of the kick and the difficulty that some may find in gaining the height and controlling the kick's impact, it is probably best to let the kick go against a glove as the high-section target. The simple drill shown below will help to develop the kick as part of a combination.

The same drill can be easily adapted for middle-section attacks.

Drill for Reverse Turning Kick

The attacker executes a rear-leg turning kick to a high-section target and …

… lands foot to foot, pivoting immediately to …

… execute a reverse turning kick to the same target.

118

10 Jumping Kicks

'Jumping kicks – effective?' may well be the reaction of martial artists from disciplines other than Taekwon-Do, but there are two good reasons why they are included here – one obvious and specific to Taekwon-Do and the other more general.

Aerial kicks lie at the heart of Taekwon-Do as they demonstrate the ultimate prowess of an exponent of a martial art with a strong emphasis on kicking and this is reflected in the scoring system where a jumping kick to the head scores the maximum available three points. That you can score the equivalent of three punches or three middle-section kicks with a single technique clearly makes jumping kicks particularly effective in Taekwon-Do sparring, but, even in the absence of such a points advantage, they can play a key role in wider sparring. Jumping kicks are powerful techniques in themselves that have the added advantage of surprise, but they are also intimidating for your opponent: when you are on the receiving end of a well executed jumping kick, aside from any concern about the blow itself, you are being made aware that your opponent is not only highly skilled but also that he feels confident enough to try out his more 'elaborate' techniques against you.

In sparring competitions, the success of fighters with jumping kicks generally relates to those that are relatively easy to perform yet can be delivered with the maximum amount of deception, and this tends to favour jumping kicks that have an element of 'spinning' in them. Why is this? Two reasons: first, it is easier to gain height (and, if required, distance) by turning the body as you jump, and, secondly, although it is slower than jumping straight up, it is more confusing for your opponent to be faced with a spinning attacker and this helps to compensate for the relative lack of speed. This section therefore focuses on three core jumping kicks that exhibit these qualities and deliver most success on the Taekwon-Do competition circuit. Although introducing jumping kicks may seem somewhat adventurous for the less experienced fighters, it is something worth persevering with, not only because it will improve your kicking technique, but also because it will increase your confidence in your own abilities ... and who would not want to look that good?

180-Degree Turning Kick

By far the most popular scoring jumping kick on the circuit today is a jumping spinning turning kick that is executed with a step and a partial or full rotation of the body in the air as the kick is delivered. The reason for the success of the kick is simple: when delivered correctly and with the appropriate timing it is extremely difficult to read because its turning motion starts on the ground (although, less practically for sparring, this and the rest of the kick can all be performed in the air), and this captures your opponent's attention. Furthermore, the motion could develop into a number of possible techniques or moves, the least likely of which to occur to your opponent is a jumping kick. There are a number of variants of the kick depending on the degree of rotation of the body – the simplest version (and most practicable for sparring) is where the body rotates 180 degrees in the air.

The fastest version of the jumping spinning turning kick and the easiest to master, the 180-degree jumping turning kick is highly deceptive

180-Degree Turning Kick

From a sparring stance, draw the front foot across the body to the open side, slightly beyond the line of the rear foot and turn the body in the same direction.

Continue turning by pivoting on the ball of the front foot, raising the rear foot off the ground and looking over the rear shoulder until facing away from the opponent.

As the turn accelerates, raise the rear leg, jump off the front foot and swap legs forcefully to execute the turning kick with the front foot before the rear foot touches the ground.

when performed at speed and it should become one of your core kicking techniques (*see* above).

Although delivered in the air, the turning kick itself is identical in form its middle- and high-section targets to the lead-leg turning kick described in Chapter 8.

Use

Since the 180-degree turn does not move you either forward or backward, the range of the kick is the same as for the normal lead-leg turning kick – the difference is in the best opportunity on which to throw the kick. Although the kick takes relatively longer than all non-jumping kicks (and, indeed, most jumping kicks) and does not alter your range, if you make use of its deceptive qualities it can be a highly effective counter-attack. This is best achieved by delivering it against a static target when your opponent is least expecting it. Clearly it is unlikely that your opponent will be 'expecting' a 180-degree jumping turning kick

(unless, of course, you throw it too many times), but he will be expecting it even less if he is looking for something else, and this is the condition that you need to try to create. The ideal use of the kick is directly after stopping your opponent's advance by blocking his attack and when he is preparing for a more 'routine' counter-attack (*see* first sequence opposite).

Alternatively, you can use your opponent's expectation of your performing the same moves to create an opening, a good example being throwing it as a counter-attack after retreating one or more steps (*see* second sequence opposite).

Practice

As important as the delivery of the kick itself is perfecting the rhythm of the turn and the kick so that it becomes a single, smooth, integrated motion and this requires many repetitions – this simple drill focuses on the rapid delivery of multiple kicks (*see* first sequence on page 122).

180-Degree Turning Kick after Blocking

As the defender steps in to block the attacker's turning kick, his front foot is already in position to start to …

… pivot round on his front foot and then …

… switch legs to deliver the kick with the lead leg.

180-Degree Turning Kick after Retreat

As the attacker continues his advance with a turning kick, he …

… interprets the defender's pivot as a continuation of his retreat, leaving …

… him unprepared for the 180-degree turning kick.

Drill for 180-Degree Turning Kick

After delivering the kick against a target on one side …

… switch stance and pivot on the other foot to …

… kick on the other side.

Back Kick

The jumping back kick adds a greater element of surprise to the speed and directness of the standard back kick, particularly when it is executed on the spot where the standard Taekwon-Do technique for jumping from a static stance is used.

The purpose of this technique is to produce the maximum height and speed with minimum initial preparatory motion when delivering a jumping kick from a standing position (usually from a fairly short and narrow stance). When perfected, it allows you to deliver jumping kicks with the maximum surprise value, and this is particularly

Taekwon-Do Jumping Technique

From a sparring stance, bend the knees slightly and …

… powerfully extend the legs to jump straight up …

… drawing the legs up towards the body at the apex of the jump.

Jumping Back Kick

With a slight bend
of the knees …

… jump straight up,
twisting in the air towards
the open side …

… to deliver the back kick
at the apex of the jump.

true of the jumping back kick where the jump is further 'disguised' by incorporating the twist of the back kick.

With all of the attributes of a standard back kick, the jumping back kick is the straight-line jumping kick of choice on the competition circuit today and it not only offers a greater level of surprise but also scores an extra point (*see* sequence above).

Use

This is an excellent, instant, counter-attacking kick that is best delivered in similar circumstances to the standard back kick (*see* sequence below).

Jumping Back Kick Counter-Attack

As the attacker starts to
advance, the defender
prepares to …

… jump and turn to …

… deliver a jumping back
kick counter as the attacker
finishes his step forwards.

Drill for Jumping Back Kick

As the opponent advances ...

... the kicker prepares to jump ...

... and kicks the opponent's target with jumping back kick.

Practice

The same basic drill as for the standard back kick will help to develop your range and timing (*see* sequence above).

Reverse Turning Kick

The jumping reverse turning kick is a technically difficult kick in two ways: first, it requires good hip flexibility to be able to perform it (particularly against a high-section target) and, secondly, it is even more difficult to control than the standard reverse turning kick. For both of these reasons the kick is seldom seen in competition sparring, but, when it is, it always receives the approval of the spectators who appreciate not only its technical difficulty but also the sheer audacity and exuberance of the fighter throwing

Jumping Reverse Turning Kick

Jumping from a sparring stance ...

... as the body turns, extend the rear leg straight out from the body ...

... and swing the heel of the kicking leg into the target.

it. How might this relate to effective Taekwon-Do sparring? Surely exhibitionism has no place in such a regime? While it is true that the objective is to win by scoring more points than your opponent and that this could be achieved merely by throwing punches, there is also room for winning in style, for pushing yourself towards a greater mastery of your martial art. For most club-level fighters the jumping reverse turning kick is something to strive for rather than a technique that can be put to use straight away and that is the spirit in which you should incorporate this technique into your training and, eventually, your sparring.

The kick is used to its best advantage against a high-section target (*see* second sequence opposite).

Use

Of all the possible instant attacks that you can throw immediately when the bout starts, this is the best since it not only scores three points but it also gives your opponent plenty to start thinking about from the outset. But otherwise, its use is similar to that of the standard reverse turning kick, that is, as a counter-intuitive technique thrown during a moment's hesitation by your opponent (*see* sequence below).

Practice

Again, a basic drill must be practised to master the kick – once you can repeatedly kick your partner's glove held at head height then you can start thinking about how you might use it in sparring and develop the appropriate drills.

Opportunity for Jumping Reverse Turning Kick

As soon as the opponent hesitates at a reasonable distance, the attacker starts to jump and turn to deliver …

… a jumping reverse turning kick to the opponent's high section on his open side.

Part III
Strategy

Effective Taekwon-Do sparring requires more than just physical prowess and a desire to win, it also requires intelligence. Each opponent will be different and even those that you spar with regularly have the potential to behave differently each time you meet – you cannot rely on the same basic game plan every time you spar. Just as in a game of chess each move that your opponent makes can change the course of the fight – you need to analyse your opponent continually, assess his strengths and weaknesses and plan accordingly. You need to develop an on-going strategy every time you fight but, unlike in chess, you must do this while instantly reacting to your opponent's moves. Such a strategy will, of course, be unique to yourself since it will rely on your individual powers of observation, experience and personality, but it must answer some fundamental questions: what type of fighter is your opponent? How can you create good openings to attack? What attacking combinations and counter-attacks will be the most successful? This part focuses on these and other issues to provide the building blocks that you can then use to develop your own successful fighting strategies.

11 Your Opponent

What are you thinking when you step on to the mat to face your opponent? The chances are that you are thinking about aspects of your strategy for the fight that is about to start, even if it may only be 'I'm going to throw my favourite technique as soon as I can', or perhaps a more complex check-list of favourite combinations that you like to throw in particular situations. It is only natural that you should have some sense of a plan for the fight, but until you have more information about your opponent, your plan is merely an aspiration. This is the crucial difference between an ideal-ized plan and an effective strategy: the former being how you would like the fight to proceed and the latter using knowledge of your opponent to devise the most effective tactics that you can use to defeat him.

Your problem is that you have only a very short time in which to assess your opponent and then to develop a strategy that can take advantage of what you have learned because Taekwon-Do sparring bouts comprise between one and three rounds, each usually lasting 2min. It is easy to over-complicate this assessment process by, for instance, trying to categorize your opponent too finely (for instance, is he a puncher, kicker, 'sniper', 'trapper' or 'faker'?) or too closely com-paring his physical attributes with your own (is he shorter, taller, thinner, fatter, weaker or stron-ger?), and much of the literature on this subject also tends to do so. The authors believe that a more pragmatic approach is required, where your assessment is limited by the time available, where you try and answer a few very basic questions as quickly as possible before going on to act deci-sively on the answers – you simply do not have the time to observe your opponent closely and then to

examine multiple options carefully. This chapter describes this cut-down assessment process, what these few key questions are and how to answer them.

Testing Your Opponent

How much can you tell from a person's body lan-guage? Probably quite a lot, but how much can you tell when that person is an opponent that you have not met before, typically in a competition, and one you are just about to face up, bow and start to fight with? Not much, given that you are both probably trying to project an impression that each wants the other to gain and that you are not in the best situation to carry out accurate psychological profiling. Before the fight starts you cannot rely on body language or other signs that can be faked – all you can do is make a physi-cal assessment of your opponent. And here again you need to guard against drawing false conclu-sions. You cannot tell how fast, strong, flexible or talented an opponent may be just by looking at him – there are some strong, smaller fighters just as there are some fast, larger ones. Since you do not know anything about your opponent's fight-ing abilities, it is by far the best option to give him your respect from the start and assume that he is a competent fighter in all regards, whether he is bigger or smaller, older or younger. Really, there is only one piece of physical information that you can glean that may be of value and that is his range – if he is significantly taller than you and he takes advantage of his greater reach then you will need to get inside his kicking range to score.

In practice, you are going to be able to assess your opponent's fighting style and abilities only once the fight starts and the authors advocate that you consciously use the early stages of the fight to 'ask' your questions by 'testing' your opponent. There are a number of reasons for this approach. One is practical in that, at the very start, two unfamiliar opponents will (generally) spend some time 'feeling' each other out before launching serious attacks and this gives you the opportunity to execute techniques or moves that test your opponent's reaction without, perhaps, as strong a response as they might later receive. Also, while your opponent is relatively static is a good opportunity to assess his stance, guard and movement since it is much harder to do so when you are reacting to his attacks and looking for openings for your own. Another important reason is to give yourself a structure to the fight where there is a finite period for assessment after which you get on with the business of winning – a prolonged wait-and-see approach will almost always lead to defeat. Additionally, this structure will, over time, increase your self-confidence since you are pursuing your strategy right from the referee's command to start, you are not passive and you are making a decision about how to proceed and acting on it.

How much time do you have? To some extent this is determined by your opponent since if he is pushing you back with 'serious' techniques then the time for asking questions is over, but, in any case, you should spend no longer (and preferably less) than 15sec testing him, leaving you at least 1min 45sec of the round to act on what you have learned. Fifteen seconds is not long, so you need to keep your questions simple and to a minimum within the following three broad categories.

Opening Moves

What are the first things that your opponent does after the command to start? Again you should avoid trying to read too much into your opponent's opening moves since he is most likely starting his own testing of you, but there are two specific things you should look for in the opening second or two of the fight.

Attack

If your opponent opens with a purposeful (rather than a feinting or testing) attack then he is probably an attacking fighter who likes to come forward. The stronger and bolder his opening attack is, for instance, a jump punch or a jumping reverse turning kick, then the more he is trying to intimidate you from the start and to dominate the fight by putting you (and, most likely, keeping you) on the defensive. How you handle an aggressive opening attack is crucial to the rest of the fight and the strategy is simple: do not be intimidated. Always be prepared for such an opening by maintaining a strong guard right from the start, avoid the attack if you can and if you can't then stand your ground, cover up and absorb it – in either case try to counter as strongly and as quickly as you can. The sooner that you show your opponent that you can give as good as you get, then the less confident he will be in his ability to dominate.

However, immediate attack can often be a standard opening move that fighters are taught to use in order to try to intimidate their opponents, so if the attack lacks power or conviction then your opponent may not be as effective an attacking fighter as he is trying to suggest, or the attack is part of his testing of you. Also, look at his reaction after the attack has been thrown and you have dealt with it: if he backs off and does not follow it up then you can draw the same conclusion.

Defence

If your opponent (like most fighters) does not open with an immediate attack, then now is a good opportunity to look at his defence, particularly since many fighters adopt their 'best' guard and stance once they have heard the referee's command to start. Try to compare your opponent's guard and stance with what you now understand to be a good defensive position, for instance:

- Is his chin covered? If it is then he is someone who thinks about his defence (although not necessarily one that fights defensively) and you are going to have to get him to drop that guard to create high-section opportunities.

- What is his body orientation? If he is square then you could have greater success with middle-section piercing kicks, if he is angled and covered up then less so.
- What direction is his rear foot facing? If it is facing to the side then he will have more trouble stepping backwards, and if his weight is also more on the back foot he will telegraph his stepping forward more.
- Is he in motion? If he is constantly, for instance, using knee flexion, he will be hard to read, but if he has static periods, even if only for a few seconds, then you may be able to take advantage of this tendency.

Also, watch to see whether his guard has a tendency to drop of its own accord (a very common fault) soon after his 'best' position – this will be exaggerated when he is attacking or defending, creating good opportunities for you.

Of course, just because he doesn't adopt a good guard so start with does not necessarily mean that he has a poor defence since good fighters will often hold their hands low to tempt their opponents to come forward and rely on evasion and greater hand speed for defence; at club-level sparring this is unlikely to be the case, but make sure to test the defence early on when facing an unknown fighter with no apparent guard.

Reactivity

How reactive is your opponent? Specifically, how does he respond to sudden movements, to feinting? The more your opponent reacts instinctively to the early stages of an attack or a feint then the better it is for you and you need to find this out as soon as possible by feinting in the opening seconds of the bout. Yet this seemingly simple thing is in fact quite difficult to do; for a feint to elicit a reaction it must be convincing and timed correctly – and being able to feint well is a key tool in the assessment process. Two kinds of feint are particularly useful when you first square up to your opponent.

Body Feint

This is the best test of your opponent's general level of reactivity because it does not feint any

Body Feint

From a sparring stance …	… move the body forward rapidly by slightly bending the lead knee and (optionally) slipping the front foot forward an inch or two.	Then, equally rapidly, move the body back to create …	… a rapid jerking movement to capture the opponent's attention.

129

particular technique or step and is therefore more a test of his general 'nervousness' and it should be the first feint that you try. The feint involves a rapid movement, almost a jerk, of the whole body in a forward direction and back again without a change in the rear foot position (*see* sequence on page 129).

To provoke the desired reaction the movement must not only be big enough and fast enough to register with your opponent, but it must also surprise him and this requires good timing on your part. You need to execute the feint when you are both relatively static since the movement would be 'lost' when you have just completed another move and it would be less noticeable to your opponent if he is in motion himself. Also, you need to feint when it is most likely to register in his peripheral vision, ideally when you are holding his gaze and he is not looking straight at any part of your body. This is a technique that you can only really practice when you are sparring – when you can consistently get a noticeable reaction from your opponent then you will know that you are doing it correctly (*see* sequence below).

Not every fighter will react to this feint but, if your opponent does, then it will be a useful opening for attacks throughout the fight; if he

does not then you may have more success with a technique feint.

Technique Feint

Here you are testing the extent to which your opponent reacts in the early stages of a specific attack by feinting a hand or leg technique. Again, to be effective the feint must be convincing and, rather than thinking of it as a technique in its own right, it is probably better to think of it as a properly executed technique that you pull back from once you have shown enough of it for your opponent to register. As with the body feint, sparring experience will tell you how much of the technique you need to show, but the timing is the same in that you want to execute the feint when there is not much else going on that might divert your opponent's attention. The major difference is in the reaction that you are seeking to provoke, which is the extent to which you can draw his guard (*see* sequence opposite).

The level of reaction will vary from fighter to fighter and also from where your opponent perceives the attack to be coming and its intended target, but any reaction, even if it is only a momentary diversion of attention, is useful and can create opportunities throughout the fight.

Desired Reaction from Body Feint

From a static position, a sudden forward movement can produce …

… a slight reaction where the opponent's guard momentarily opens out a little.

Desired Reaction from Technique Feint

Feinting a high-section punch draws the opponent's guard up creating …

… an opportunity for a middle-section attack such as a back kick.

Resilience

How resilient is your opponent? Testing your opponent with a strong technique in the early stages will not only tell you a lot about him but it will also tell him something about *you*. If your opponent shows a good defence but has neither come forward nor backed off significantly towards the end of your testing period and you are still unclear as to what kind of fighter he is, then throwing a single, solid technique, such as a rear-leg turning kick to his middle section, is a useful final test before you turn to the business of scoring points. Your opponent can react in one of three ways to such a technique delivered with some power against his guard:

- He backs off or 'drops' further behind his guard – if he shows obvious discomfort without reply, even though you have not scored, then he is already lapsing into a defensive mode and you should continue to press your attack.
- He replies immediately – while he is not intimidated by you, if he replies in kind then he can be provoked, which is a trait that you should be able to take advantage of.

- He stands his ground – if he absorbs the kick without apparent concern since he knows it has not scored, then he is neither intimidated nor provoked and you need to start sparring in earnest in order to read him further.

If nothing else, at least your opponent knows from the start that you can deliver techniques with power which will, you hope, make him proceed a little more cautiously.

Assessment

You have had an, albeit brief, chance to assess your opponent using some or all of the techniques described above and you will have noted some important aspects of your opponent's style and approach that you may be able to use to your advantage and some that you may need to watch out for – but what general conclusions can you draw to help you to win the fight? Again, over-analysis is unhelpful here and your strategy going forward will be determined by two principal considerations, one on the basis of your initial assessment and one as the fight develops.

Appetite

Your opponent's opening moves and his reactions to yours give you an insight into his general 'appetite' for the fight such as his desire to get started, his degree of nervousness and his level of concern about being hit. To put it bluntly: to what extent is he 'up for it'? If you are faced with an opponent who looks in any way uncomfortable about fighting you, then the door is open for you to try and dominate him and control the fight and this should be the basis of your opening strategy. This is, of course, subject to the proviso that appetite is not the same as ability and it is possible that your opponent is, for instance, highly skilled but naturally nervous; however, it is nonetheless best to press your attacks and see whether or not his appetite increases.

On the other hand, if your opponent seems comfortable and confident then you really need to find out (if you have not done so already) what type of fighter he is, which should become evident after the first tentative steps and as the fight gets into full swing.

Attacker or Counter-Attacker?

Against a confident and (assumedly) competent opponent, there is one key question about his fighting style that needs to be answered and that is whether he tends to come forward as an aggressive attacking fighter or if he likes to draw you into his counter-attacks. Most competent fighters will employ both approaches, but if he shows a marked preference for either, then this, more than any other type-casting, will affect your strategy for the fight.

Attacker

As previously stated, you must not be intimidated by a strong attacking opponent and you must assert yourself early in the fight in two ways: first, you need to throw some powerful techniques quickly – even if they do not score, your opponent needs to know that you can hit hard and that there will be a price to be paid for advancing into your kicking and punching ranges. Second, you must avoid lapsing into the role that is being presented to you (that is, of being predominantly defensive) by pressing forward with your own attacks and combinations. Both these strategies can seem difficult when you are on the receiving end of multiple flurries of attacks from a strong opponent and, sometimes, he will simply be better than you are, but it is important that you try hard to limit his dominance – you can only improve by pitting yourself against better fighters. Also dominating fighters become used to their fights following a predictable pattern – if you can break this pattern, you may be surprised at the opportunities that flow from it.

Counter-Attacker

Conversely, a skilled counter-attacker with good defensive skills can be a very frustrating opponent where you can seem to be putting in all of the effort but he is reaping the rewards – here you need to use more guile and try to use the same counter-attacking skills against him. Is there a pattern to your opponent's counter-attacking? Does he tend to counter-attack particular techniques of yours and does he use particular techniques to counter with? Most counter-attackers like to score early in your advance and then back off, so, rather than concentrating on launching straightforward combinations of attacks against your opponent, use your observations of his counter-attacking style to try to attack in two stages. First, launch your initial attack to draw his counter and then, secondly, try to immediately and strongly counter-attack his technique. This will undermine his counter-attacking strategy since, even if you do not score with the first technique, if you have correctly anticipated his counter then you are in a good position to score with the second thereby at least levelling the score in the exchange.

12 Creating Openings

When is the best time to launch an attack? Right at the start of the fight? When your opponent is advancing or retreating? At close range or long range? There is no single right answer, it all depends on the circumstances at the time, but there is a time when your attack is always less likely to succeed: when your opponent is expecting it. When you are facing an opponent with a strong guard (and perhaps good counter-attacking skills) then, unless you are deliberately attacking his guard to provoke a reaction, he is unlikely to be bothered by your attack and you are merely wasting energy. This not to say that a fast attack cannot score against a well defended opponent, but it is going to be more likely to succeed if you can either divert him momentarily from his expectations or throw a technique other than the one he is expecting. This is what an opening is: the recognition of or the creation of an opportunity to launch an attack against a weakness in your opponent's defence or with an increased element of surprise. The ability to create and exploit openings is a critical component of effective sparring – to be able to catch your opponent off guard with the appropriate technique is at least as important as the quality of the technique itself.

There are, of course, many possible openings and ways to create them and you will find and develop those that work best for you with your favourite techniques, but they will generally fall into the three categories presented below, along with some useful examples to get you started.

Reaction

By far the simplest way to create an opening is to provoke a reaction in your opponent – that moment of tension and indecision that follows a sudden movement or feint on your part. Feinting was covered in some detail in the preceding chapter as a good way to test your opponent's reactivity, but it takes fast reactions and good timing on your part to take advantage of such fleeting opportunities.

What does not work is if you perform everything sequentially: you decide that now is a good moment to feint your opponent, you do so, he reacts, you note his reaction and decide which attack to launch, and so on. You just do not have the time – your opponent's reaction is likely to last less than a second and within that second your attack needs to be on its way if it is to take advantage of any momentary confusion, otherwise it is too late. Therefore, if you want to attack after a feint it is best to know in advance which technique or combination you are going to follow up with and that attack (or first technique in the combination) needs to be launched while the reaction to the feint is taking place.

While any technique can potentially take advantage of the reaction to a feint, because the attack immediately following a feint needs to be fast the most popular ones tend to be punching techniques and short-range kicks. Two representative and highly effective feint and attack combinations that are likely to score immediately are presented in detail below in order to get you thinking about what else might work for you in similar situations.

Body Feint and Switch Turning Kick

This seemingly simple technique compounds the reaction to the feint with a 'surprise' attack, the switch turning kick that, like the switch back kick

Switch Turning Kick

Sharply raise the lead leg while jumping off …

… the back leg and turning the hips in the air to deliver …

… a turning kick with the rear leg.

described in Chapter 9, is a fast yet deceptive, shorter-range kick (*see* sequence above).

The speed and confusion of the kick allows the attacker to take advantage of the reaction to a body feint (*see* sequence below).

But it is more than just speed that makes the switch turning kick so effective after a successful body feint – the choice of technique is difficult for the defender to predict for two reasons: at close range he assumes that a punch is more likely than a kick and, given the range, if a kick were coming it would more likely be a lead-leg kick. This combination of speed and surprise makes the most of the opening created by the feint and the chances of scoring much higher – try and work these principles into your own feint and attack scenarios.

Body Feint and Middle-Section Switch Turning Kick

While defender is still reacting to the feint …

… the attacker jumps to deliver …

… a middle-section switch turning kick.

Kick Feint and Punch

Working on the same principles as the blitz reverse punch described in Chapter 7, this technique uses the feet to distract attention from the hands by feinting a side kick to draw your opponent's guard downwards to set him up for a high-section punch (*see* sequence below).

Again, it is worth analysing why this popular feint and attack combination is so effective and the primary reason is in the choice of the feint. By drawing the lead leg across the body, your opponent registers that it is not likely to develop into a lead-leg turning kick but that it will most likely become a side kick or perhaps a hooking kick. This provides a double benefit in that not only is his attention drawn towards a potential kick, but also that enough of the kick has been 'revealed' to, one hopes, draw his guard away from the very area that you want to attack. The lesson here is that, while a technique feint can be little more than a sharp movement of an attacking limb that provokes a minimal reaction, a more specific feint can create a correspondingly more specific and often greater reaction that can in turn create a better opening for a particular attack.

Diversion

An opponent with good defensive skills will normally try and 'dictate' his body orientation towards you, regardless of whether he is attacking or defending, that is, he will try and face you with his body at his preferred angle relative to yours. This can create a problem for you, particularly if your opponent is not susceptible to feints and maintains a strong guard, in that you are always trying to create openings against his 'best' defensive position. In this situation you need to disrupt your opponent's composure and break his dominance in setting your relative positions by diverting him from his normal straight-line advance and retreat movements behind his guard. You need to get him to move 'out of character' by taking over the 'direction agenda' and forcing him to react to your own, particularly lateral and diagonal, movements. Your diversion objectives are two-staged: first, to position yourself so that you can get around your opponent's guard to create a scoring opportunity, and, second, to get him to follow your movements, break his rhythm and make him change his body orientation. The former is

Kick Feint and Punch

The attacker's side/hooking kick feint draws down the defender's guard providing a …

… brief opening for a cross punch to the defender's high section.

covered in Chapter 5, where diagonal shuffling, side-stepping and splitting to the side are all useful tactics for getting around your opponent's guard, while the latter, orientation change, seeks to create an opening as your opponent changes direction and is covered below.

In some ways this can be considered as an extension of a feint in that, instead of seeking to provoke a momentary reaction, you are trying to provoke your opponent to move (or start to move), usually laterally or diagonally – your opportunity comes as he starts to move off the horizontal path to return to his preferred orientation to you. This is unlikely to happen on your first change of direction since, if your opponent turned quickly enough to avoid your getting around his guard, you will then be too late to catch him in transition – you need to link more than one lateral or diagonal movement together by, for example, side-stepping and jumping diagonally (*see* sequence below).

Side Stepping and Jumping Diagonally

From a sparring stance, quickly ...

... side-step to the open side and then ...

... immediately jump diagonally with a jumping reverse punch.

From a relatively close distance ...

... the defender's 'out of character' side-step is difficult for the defender to interpret and the moment of indecision allows the attacker to ...

... penetrate the side of his guard with the jumping punching coming from the diagonal.

There are, of course, almost limitless possibilities for achieving your objective of creating an opening by diverting your opponent and you will develop your own techniques over time, but be sure to try to vary the speed and direction of your movements – a slower movement followed by a rapid movement, as in the example above, is often successful but do not use the same diversionary tactic too often or you will find him 'training' you.

Training

When facing a reasonably evenly matched opponent, particularly one who fights in a similar style to yourself, it can seem difficult to find a way of creating an opening by forcing him to react to your feints and movements and it often pays dividends to try and spot patterns in his behaviour that you can exploit. If he has a favourite technique that you can predict then you have an opening to use a specific counter-attack, as described in Chapter 14 and the same is true if you can spot a particular pattern of movement, either advancing or retreating, initiated by your opponent or in response to your own actions. The term 'training' is used in this context because, once you spot the pattern of behaviour that creates an opportunity to attack, then you want to get your opponent to repeat it.

The first problem is to recognize the pattern of behaviour in the limited time available. Since you do not have the time nor the level of concentration to undertake any kind of 'study' after the initial assessment of your opponent, your starting point should be the most common sequences of movements, for example, advancing and retreating in a straight line. Does your opponent tend to try to fill the 'gap' when you are retreating and maintain it when you are advancing? This is an extremely common, and not necessarily conscious, reaction where your opponent steps forward, sees you step backwards and is drawn to take another step forward, perhaps to pursue the attack or perhaps just attracted by the lack of resistance on your part. The same is true if you step forward and your opponent's first reaction is to step backward, in that there is a significant chance that he will do the same again if you continue to step forward, but the psychology is different here – your opponent is not acting out of any sense of bravado, so beware that he is not training you for a counter-attack. Also, if he is moving back purely defensively then he will want to stop doing so as quickly as possible, making

Tempting Opponent to Step Forward

If opponent hesitates in his advance then …

… the attacker dropping his guard or …

… leaning forward can tempt the opponent to make the next step.

his period of predictable behaviour shorter and you are much more likely to have success with an appropriate combination of attacks as described in the next chapter.

Training an opponent who is advancing is easier because he is, to some extent, 'carried away' with the success of his advance and may not be thinking as clearly and cautiously as he should, he is therefore less likely to recognize that he is being trained. Using your straight-line retreat as an example, your second problem is to get him to repeat the same sequence of steps (with or without attacks) for you to take advantage of. You may be lucky and find that your opponent habitually presses forward when you retreat, but, if he exercises more caution, then you may need to tempt him to take another step after his first, for example as in the sequence on page 137.

After having retreated from your opponent once or twice, he now has an expectation that you

are going to continue to do so and the next time he takes a step forward, you retreat and, as he is just about to take another step forward, he will, you hope, be lulled into a false sense of security. This is your opening to attack – when he thinks things are following the same pattern as before and his confidence of closing his advance with a successful attack is increasing – and a perfect technique here is the back kick that takes full advantage of his forward momentum (*see* sequence below).

This is not a tactic that can be used frequently in a fight, training is nonetheless an extremely satisfying way to catch your opponent by using your intelligence as well as technique – always a useful message to send to your opponent. Watch out for other training opportunities, but always remember that time is limited and you cannot afford to wait too long for something that may not happen.

Switch Back Kick after Trained Advance

After the attacker has taken a step forward ...

... defender leans forward to tempt the attacker on to ...

... a well-timed, switch back kick.

13 Attacking Combinations

While single techniques can score against your opponent, linking techniques together in attacking combinations significantly increases your chances of scoring points in a given exchange because you are not only executing more techniques but, correctly pulled together, each technique creates better opportunities for the one that follows.

Combinations are therefore a key attacking component in effective Taekwon-Do sparring and they should be at the heart of your attacking strategy – the more good combinations you throw, the better your chances of winning.

What makes a combination work is due partly to the extent that the techniques complement each other and partly to your personal preferences and abilities. This chapter seeks to explain the former in order to help you to find or create the combinations that best suit you and your style of fighting by examining some particularly effective examples of two of the most popular types of combination: hand techniques followed by kicks and multiple kicks. This is an area where you can be as inventive as you like since you can never have enough combinations, but merely thinking of a good combination is only half the battle, you need to practise it extensively so that it becomes instinctive and can be delivered at speed. Try to develop a core of combinations that work for you and that you can throw with the same assuredness as your favourite individual techniques, then refine them and add to them as your sparring experience grows.

Punch Kick Combinations

Linking hand techniques (normally punches) with kicks forms what are arguably the most effective attacking combinations in Taekwon-Do sparring, because, aside from the merits of the particular techniques, they all draw upon the same fundamental deception: while your opponent is dealing with fast hand techniques generated at your shoulder height, he is less likely to spot kicks starting from your low section.

Jab Cross Turning Kick Combination

These combinations use the naturally fastest hand combination to push your opponent back and set him up for a long-range kick. The use of multiple punches at the start ensures that your opponent's attention is focused on your hands and not on your legs (*see* first sequence on page 140).

The key to success for this combination lies in the commitment of the punches forcing your opponent back (or at the very least drawing his guard) and in starting the kick before the cross has finished. The turning kick is particularly suitable here as its innate deceptiveness helps to disguise the kick and its long range allows you to catch your opponent even if he is retreating fast, and, if you can draw your opponent's guard towards your closed side, then you can always go for the extra point with a high-section kick (*see* second sequence on page 140).

Jab Cross Back Kick Combination

Another kick that works well with the jab and cross is the back kick that, like the turning kick, brings an additional degree of deceptiveness to the combination. It is particularly effective at extremes of distance, such as when your

Jab Cross Middle-Section Turning Kick Combination

The attacker jabs to the head and immediately follows up with a ...

... high-section cross which not only forces defender back but also draws his guard, setting him up perfectly for ...

... a rear-leg, turning kick to his exposed middle section.

Jab Cross High-Section Turning Kick Combination

The attacker's jab and ...

... cross do not force defender back but turn him on to ...

... a lead-leg kick to the high section.

Jab Cross Switch Back Kick Combination

The defender successfully parries the attacker's jab ...

... and cross, keeping the high section protected and not moving back but open to ...

... the attacker's switch back kick to the middle section.

opponent does not back off from your punches (*see* sequence above).

Equally, the back kick can be used to close a distance if your opponent retreats well out of range by using a stepping back kick (*see* sequence below).

Jumping Punch Back Kick Combination

Another combination that exploits a rapid retreat is a jumping punch followed by a back kick (*see* first sequence on page 142).

Again, as with the jab cross stepping back kick combination, for an extremely rapidly

Jab Cross Stepping Back Kick Combination

The defender parries the attacker's jab and ...

... steps back to avoid the cross as the attacker ...

... pursues the defender and closes the distance with a stepping back kick.

Jumping Punch Back Kick Combination

The defender retreats rapidly from the attacker's jumping punch and …

… the attacker closes the gap by delivering a back kick as soon as he lands.

Jumping Punch Sliding Back Kick Combination

The defender moves well out of range for the jumping punch and …

… the attacker pushes off the supporting leg to reach the defender with a …

… sliding back kick.

retreating opponent an even greater distance can be covered by using a stepping back kick or, alternatively, a sliding back kick (*see* second sequence opposite).

Reverse Punch Rear-Leg Hooking Kick Combination

Although punch kick combinations are generally used to take advantage of a retreating opponent, their fundamental deception of keeping your opponent focused on your hands and not on your feet can also be effective at closer range, although this limits the kicks that can be used. A good example of this is to use a hand technique to one side of the body, such as a reverse punch to draw attention from a kick to the other side, such as a rear-leg hooking kick (*see* first sequence below).

Although infrequently used in sparring, the reverse knife-hand strike makes a good substitute for the reverse punch, not only because its 'bigger' motion makes it even more likely to draw your opponent's guard, but also because it can

Reverse Punch Rear-Leg Hooking Kick Combination

The attacker's middle-section reverse punch draws the defender's guard down allowing …

… the attacker to come in over the top of the guard with a high-section, rear-leg hooking kick.

Reverse Knife Hand Rear-Leg Hooking Kick Combination

The attacker's reverse knife-hand strike not only diverts the defender's attention but can, if it connects, force the opponent's head on to …

… a hooking kick to the other side.

143

target the opposite side of your opponent's head (*see* second sequence on page 143).

Multiple Kick Combinations

One of the hallmarks of kick-based martial arts (and particularly Taekwon-Do) is the use of multiple kicks to break through an opponent's defences – executed correctly these can be extremely effective combinations, but they must be fast and flowing to avoid their being read by your opponent. There are two principal types of multiple kick combination: those performed consecutively with the same leg (typically without returning the kicking leg to the floor between kicks) against a shorter-range, relatively static target, and those comprising separate kicks, usually against a retreating target.

Consecutive Front Snap Kick Turning Kick Combination

This is the classic, consecutive kick combination, where the first kick draws your opponent's

Consecutive Front Snap Kick Turning Kick Combination

As the front snap kick draws the defender's guard down, the attacker needs only to partly pull back the lower leg, continue to raise the kicking leg and turn the hips to rapidly follow up with …

… a high-section turning kick.

Consecutive Side Kick Turning Kick Combination

At the correct range, the attacker's side kick is not fully extended in order to …

… be able to reach the high-section target with the consecutive turning kick.

attention down to his middle section, creating an opening for a quick change of attack to his high section (*see* first sequence opposite).

Speed is the key here, but you must not shorten the front snap kick too much in your haste to execute the turning kick or your opponent will not register the first kick and will not move his guard. This is a common error with this combination, possibly because many fighters tend not to use the front snap kick much in its own right and therefore fail to be convincing with it – a more obvious kick to draw your opponent's guard and attention is a side kick which is a useful variation of the same basic tactic (*see* second sequence opposite).

Consecutive Hooking Kick Turning Kick Combination

Instead of drawing your opponent's guard downwards, this consecutive kick combination draws his guard to one side to deliver a kick to the other (*see* sequence below).

If you have the flexibility then this can be a very deceptive and therefore effective combination; however, if you find the high-section hooking kick difficult then you could always substitute a middle-section kick to your opponent's closed side, but you still need to combine it with a high-section turning kick as, in this case, the second kick must go to his open side.

Consecutive Hooking Kick Turning Kick Combination

Again, as well as drawing the defender's guard, if the attacker connects with the hooking kick it forces the defender's head on to ...

... the attacker's consecutive turning kick to the other side of the defender's head.

Rear-Leg Turning Kick Reverse Turning Kick Combination

A powerful rear-leg, turning kick forces the defender back as …

… the attacker lands foot to foot and immediately pivots on his first kicking leg to …

… deliver a reverse turning kick with the other leg.

Rear-Leg Turning Kick 180-Degree Turning Kick Combination

After the attacker's turning kick forces the defender back …

… the attacker pivots on his front foot as soon as the kicking leg lands to deliver …

… a 180-degree jumping turning kick to the defender's middle section.

Rear-Leg Turning Kick Reverse Turning Kick Combination

This combination uses the power of the rear-leg turning kick to force your opponent backwards and then follow up with a reverse turning kick (*see* first sequence opposite).

Although both kicks are targeting the same area, the combination is effective due to the expectation of another rear-leg turning kick to your opponent's opposite side and the difficulty of reading the reverse turning kick while retreating.

Rear-Leg Turning Kick 180-Degree Turning Kick Combination

Like the previous example, this combination uses the rear-leg turning kick to push your opponent back and follows up with a similarly deceptive kick to the same side (*see* second sequence opposite).

Lead-Leg Consecutive Turning Kicks Back Kick Combination

This combination combines consecutive turning kicks to progressively raise your opponent's guard and to create an opportunity to score with the back kick (*see* sequence below).

Lead-Leg Consecutive Turning Kicks Back Kick Combination

The attacker's first turning kick to the middle section followed by ...

... a consecutive turning kick to the high section draws the defender's guard and forces him back within range of ...

... the attacker's back kick delivered with the other leg, after landing from the consecutive kicks.

14 Counter-Attacking

Although you cannot rely solely on counter-attacking and you need to go forward to win, counter-attacking is nonetheless a key component of effective sparring for two principal reasons: first, you cannot always go forward – you must sometimes defend – and if you can notch up some points from your defensive exchange then so much the better; second, and more importantly, is the disquieting effect that counter-attacking can have on your opponent – while any reply to an attack can be deemed a counter-attack, the ones that will upset your opponent the most are those that show him that you are able to 'read' him and that you have an answer to his favourite techniques. This is the purpose of this chapter: to help you to develop counter-attacks that undermine your opponent's reliance on his core techniques, the use of which you can predict with reasonable accuracy – in practice, and, at the club-fighter level, this means concentrating on kicks since they are generally slower and easier to read than punches. Presented below are examples of proven counter-attacks to the three most popular kicks used in Taekwon-Do sparring – the turning kick, the side kick and the back kick – all of which are relatively easy to predict. Study the examples carefully to gain an understanding of their timing and why they work so

Jab Cross Counter-Attack to Turning Kick

As soon as the defender covers up to absorb the high-section, turning kick, he immediately starts to counter-attack with a jab that …

… connects with the attacker as soon as he lands and is swiftly followed by …

… the defender's cross punch.

Jumping Back Fist Counter-Attack to Turning Kick

After blocking the turning kick, the defender ...

... jumps before the attacker has landed from his kick, giving the jumping back fist ...

... maximum surprise value.

that you can then apply this in modifying them to your personal style and in developing your own personal favourites. However, the prediction of your opponent's favourite kicks is down to your own powers of observation and experience – it can only really be learnt by sparring and it is a skill that you should try hard to develop each and every time you fight.

Turning Kick Counter-Attacks

The popularity of the turning kick has already been shown and it would be rare indeed to see a fight in which it did not feature, so it is essential that you have some effective counter-attacks in your armoury. Although it can be a powerful kick, it is also one of the easiest to block and absorb, which increases the short-range counter-attacking opportunities.

Hand Technique Counter-Attacks to Turning Kick

This is the classic 'stand-your-ground' counter-attack, where you can exploit your opponent's proximity and lack of a tight defence after he has completed his kick (*see* sequence opposite).

This counter-attack beautifully illustrates the value of a strong defence with its ease of blocking and the speed with which you can counter-attack.

A useful alternative to the previous counter that has the advantages of surprise and a higher scoring tariff is the jumping back fist (*see* sequence above).

Kick Counter-Attacks to Turning Kick

When the turning kick is avoided rather than blocked, a longer-range counter-attack such as the back kick can be used (*see* sequence on page 150).

Back Kick Counter-Attack to Turning Kick

By the defender's leaning back to avoid the turning kick …

… the attacker is encouraged to continue his advance and on to …

… the defender's back kick.

Again, the 'surrender' initially implied by the back kick as the body moves away from the opponent makes it a difficult counter-attack to read.

Another option is to use the momentum from the initial block to launch a powerful counter-attack (*see* first sequence opposite).

Finally, if you have the flexibility, then the deceptiveness of the hooking kick is enhanced by blocking on the opposite side (*see* second sequence opposite).

Side Kick Counter-Attacks

Unlike the turning kick, it is difficult to launch an instant counter-attack just after having absorbed a powerful side kick, and the most effective counter-attacks follow on from either deflecting

Reverse Turning Kick Counter-Attack to Turning Kick

The defender starts to pivot to block the turning kick …

… and continues the pivot to counter-attack with a high-section, reverse turning kick.

Hooking Kick Counter-Attack to Turning Kick

After blocking the turning kick …

… the hooking kick counter is seldom expected.

or avoiding the kick by side-stepping to the inside of the kick.

Hand Technique Counter-Attacks to Side Kick

The distance necessary to avoid a side kick means that you must step closer to counter-attack with a hand technique, as in this typical punching counter-attack (*see* first sequence on page 152).

Kick Counter-Attacks to Side Kick

Kick counter-attacks have the advantage that they are within range after the initial avoidance of the kick, and this counter-attack uses the commonest and most effective deflecting block for the side kick (*see* second sequence on page 152).

If the block is performed accurately, that is, at the joint of the shin and the instep, it can be quite

Reverse Punch Counter-Attack to Side Kick

The side kick is usually easier to read than most and therefore easier to avoid with a side-step to the attacker's open side …

… which is a good position to slip the front foot closer and …

… counter-attack with a high-section, reverse punch.

Rear-Leg Turning Kick Counter-Attack to Side Kick

The defender deflects the kick, turning the attacker slightly towards his closed side and …

… leaving his open side more exposed to the high-section, rear-leg turning kick counter.

disabling and it is worth perfecting for use against persistent side-kickers.

Several other kicks can be used to similar effect with the downward kick being particularly difficult to block (*see* first sequence below).

Requiring slightly less flexibility after a side-step is the hooking kick (*see* second sequence below).

If you want to go for the extra point, the jumping back kick works particularly well after the side-step (*see* first sequence on page 154).

Downward Kick Counter-Attack to Side Kick

After side-stepping …

… to avoid the kick, a slight …

… slide forward on the back foot allows the defender to counter with a downward kick.

Hooking Kick Counter-Attack to Side Kick

After side-stepping …

… counter with a lead-leg hooking kick.

Jumping Back Kick Counter-Attack to Side Kick

Side-stepping away from the side kick puts the defender in a good position to counter with …

… a jumping back kick.

Finally, if you want to go for maximum points then try a high-section, switch turning kick (*see* sequence below).

Back Kick Counter-Attacks

Of the three kicks covered here, the back kick is the hardest to block and the hardest to counter due to its power, range and the strong defensive position it offers the attacker – on the upside, however, the turning of the body to execute the kick makes it easier to read. As with the side kick, side-stepping is normally the best way to prepare for a counter-attack, but you need to try to get in a little closer to reduce the greater distance between the end of the kick and the attacker's body.

Switch Turning Kick Counter-Attack to Side Kick

As soon as the front foot has followed the rear foot in the side-step to avoid the kick …

… take off from the front foot to …

… deliver a high-section, turning kick with the rear foot in the air.

Reverse Punch Counter-Attack to Back Kick

As the attacker starts his back kick …

… the defender splits to the inside of the kick and …

… counter-attacks with a stepping punch to the side of the attacker's head.

Hand Technique Counter-Attacks to Back Kick

The simplest counter-attacks involve stepping inside the kick to counter with a punch before the attacker fully reorientates himself after kicking (*see* sequence above).

For greater speed, range and an extra point, the jumping punch is a useful alternative (*see* below).

If your opponent is particularly easy to read then it is worth trying to block the kick to further disrupt his recovery from the kick before coming straight in with a jumping punch (*see* sequence on page 156).

Jumping Punch Counter-Attack to Back Kick

The defender …

… side-steps to the inside of the attacker's back kick and …

… immediately counter-attacks with a jumping punch.

Block and Jumping Punch Counter-Attack to Back Kick

If you can stand your ground and block the kick either downwards ...

... or on the outside of the kicking leg, then you can launch ...

... straight into a jumping punch counter.

Kick Counter-Attacks to Back Kick

While side-stepping puts you in kicking range for a counter without your having to take an additional step, your target area is very limited if you side-step inside the kick and you need to be accurate with your counter-attack (*see* first sequence opposite).

Although side-stepping to the outside of your opponent's back kick requires better timing, it does offer a greater choice of target with a middle-section turning kick counter-attack to a back kick (*see* second sequence opposite).

High-Section Turning Kick Counter-Attack to Back Kick

As the attacker starts his back kick …

… the defender splits to the inside of the kick and …

… counter-attacks with a stepping kick to the side of the attacker's head.

Middle-Section Turning Kick Counter-Attack to Back Kick

Side-stepping …

… to the outside of the attacker's kick makes …

… the middle section a viable target for a rear-leg, turning kick counter-attack.

Index

Entries in *italic* refer to photographic illustrations.